DIGITAL CONTENT
MANAGEMENT

How to Easily Transform Your
Marketing with the Tools of the
Digital, Social and Virtual World and
Attract Only Already Interested
Customers

Matthew K. Atkins

Digital Content Management

Copyright © 2020 Matthew K. Atkins

Printed by Line Profile Ed.

First printing, June 2020.

Line Profile Ed.

https://www.lineprofile.net

Table of Contents

Preface

The changes in the world we live in are subtle, almost imperceptible. Yet, today many of our customs have radically changed. Thanks to an invisible network that previously only served to connect us, but today it has matured and has become capable of giving us advice, of simplifying our daily lives. How has all this been possible in such a short time? Who allowed this to happen? And now that all this has become customary, what can we do, rebel, or adapt to new technologies?

Let's take a step back. Our society is complex, many of the certainties of the past have failed, and perhaps we found ourselves in a condition of profound crisis precisely for this reason. Economic crisis, model crisis, the crisis of old industrial realities that have failed to understand that change was upon us and that we needed to adapt and take necessary countermeasures in time. Many companies did not want to ride the change; because of this they were left behind and were sometimes forced to choose between repositioning themselves in "more traditional" markets or to fail miserably.

But which markets can resist the new world if the same distribution is slowly but surely passing into the hands of other operators? Which traditional businesses can feel protected from technological innovations that change old conventions every day, eradicate customs, completely change people's points of view and way of thinking?

Furthermore, our society presents very complex stratification, where completely different dimensions and situations coexist on different time planes*. Like in a large transit station, we can observe the passing of very fast trains that enter at a crazy speed without even stopping, or stop just a few moments; oil-powered regional trains traveling on non-electrified lines; a subway train; a surface tram that continues its ride through the city and even a steam locomotive used for touristic itineraries. All these convoys might be crossing the same station at the same time, but each one will be traveling at a different speed and for different purposes. The same happens in our society: unlike in the past, each generation has a range of customs and exigencies that intersect with completely different problems characterizing those preceding it and the ones that will follow.

This example is important to try to correctly interpret our world, and not to find us unprepared.

Our liquid society, made out of unstable and temporary structures, of a continuous transformation, of perennial precariousness, can demolish consolidated businesses in the blink of an eye; but on the other hand, it also allows us to easily create new ones in very little time. Hence, we should not fear this kind of society; instead, we need to understand its dynamics and foresee what the next trends will be in order to obtain profit from them. We shall, therefore, leave the sense of uncertainty, the fear of constantly changing realities and of the rise of new dynamics aside, and face the present with the courage necessary to carry out new ideas and projects. Fortunately, today we are not alone, or at least, we are certainly less alone than before, as we have an important number of tools available that allow us to program, monitor, test, validate, and advertise our business.

In this book, we deal with the relationship between business networks and the digital world. The internet revolution has outlined entirely new scenarios, which were inconceivable until a few years ago. The internet, the revolutionary concept of the hyperlink -i.e. an arc connecting two nodes- has allowed humans, and now also machines, to stay connected and turn the world into a global village inhabited by individuals, real objects and virtual objects. We can discover places that are situated on the other side of the Earth, tools of every kind are available in the cloud, people are represented by avatars and we are able to travel to new dimensions. However, we must always be careful to critically evaluate whether this new world is objectively interesting and suitable for developing projects or it is formed by empty rooms, virtual copies of places and activities we were used to in the past and that someone has thought to replicate in the virtual world, without knowing if they could be as stimulating for the human mind as the real ones were. The concern that this new land can be eliminated with the mere click of a mouse remains, as well as the uncertainty that the platforms we deal with will continue to be used in the future. This is why our gaze must be critical, our assessment attentive to understanding the new world with a good measure of realism.

Introduction

We suddenly decided to transfer many of the activities that we consider as habits -such as listening to a good record, leafing through a book, going in search of a good restaurant, going to the hospital- to a new space that was apparently invisible, but which can always present itself in a new shape, be it an image, a sound, or a service based on the instrument we use to consult it: "the network of networks". We can ask questions or talk to some device near to us, citing the name of the song we want to listen to, and our favorite music will immediately start in the background; we can ask a smartphone to take us to the best seafood restaurant nearby, and our wish will be granted. What a strange world, made of new, invisible realities controlled by a single large system able to know where we are, what our habits are, to understand where we are presumably going, or to suggest what to do in the evening! And we are only at the beginning of an expanding reality that will lead to the subverting of all human certainties. If these tools are already part of our real life, we must assume that they have been developed to do business, to better exploit markets; hence, it would be reasonable to ask ourselves if by knowing them better, we could also take advantage of the potential of the network to build or improve the performance of our business.

This book aims to thoroughly document all the opportunities offered by digital services but to do that with a good measure of criticism, which we'll often find useful during our work. The internet was the starting point for countless further applications that have been developed over time and have innovated our way of living and behaving. Search engines were initially born to index what was gradually being created in the internet world. Blogs were born later to create ever new content, and in their wake social networks have succeeded in linking such contents to people and building communities of people who share friendship, kinship, passions, and knowledge. Today, the virtual world has reached an important level of development and is strongly advancing in the real world. As proof of this, smart glasses and visors have been designed, and apps that contemplate augmented reality are multiplying. Movies produced with the aid of the newest technologies already project us into places where it becomes almost impossible to distinguish between the real world and the virtual one, and probably, humanity will gradually but surely enter the new era they describe. This may appear to be an apocalyptic scenario, but the new generations seem to be dealing with this new dimension quite well. It may happen that someone hits a pole while walking looking at the cell phone, but surely my 9-year-old son has more computer skills than my father, who worked forty years at IBM. If anything, for those of us who want to understand the advantages of the newest available tools, who want to develop new business ideas or to seize digital opportunities to strengthen our professional activities, it is appropriate to take stock of the situation. We must understand which the best tools are, how simple or complex they are to use, what the future prospects of the big companies in the digital world can be and what space will be left to free initiative. In the next chapters, we will eventually discover that today, it is possible to build a business without activation costs or initial investments. Once, in fact, those who wanted to open a shop or an office had to find appropriate locations, warehouses, buy or rent them, restructure them, and the activity could not ignore objective management limits. Today, free from the four walls, immersed in a virtual world, it is possible to conceive the creation of multiple activities that simultaneously exploit different markets and constantly evolve. If we can understand what these mechanisms are, perhaps we can try to adapt them to a family business, to data mining work, or to the realization of our business ideas. A business that, as it is conceived, can only be liquid!

With this book, we want to provide a method, a tactic, a real scheme to consistently develop a business that can become successful without a considerable initial investment. We will choose the best apps on the internet and use them to get the maximum benefits. We do not want to be overwhelmed by innovation, but to manage it to our advantage. We do not want to play the part of the victims in a society that no longer recognizes itself in any defined scheme, but to be the main characters of this new world.

This book also wants to be a key to understanding the new world; in order to fully exploit the resources that are available, being able to search for a word on Google or post a photo on Facebook is not enough: rather, we should have the required technical tools at hand to understand how we can manage the parallel, digital world in a better way. The revolution that was started by the creation of the internet has now reached its peak and the future of business and economy cannot ignore what has been done so far to turn the real world into a virtual one.

At first, it was with vinyl records, which could be called analog technology; then they became CDs and then DVDs. Today, we know that physical support is no longer needed to listen to music. Something similar happened for photography: we went from photographic film and silver halide chemistry to digital sensors that have transformed an image into a matrix of numbers -and as you probably know, numbers are easy to share through a flow of data.

It is only a matter of time: everything that can be transformed into a digital medium, i.e. numbers and letters, will leave the Earth to live on a server. We should no longer be surprised by the wonders of this new universe, where even emotions can be managed digitally. When I receive a congratulatory notification for my contribution offered by posting photos of the places I visit

I am flattered. That email was automatically generated by a robot. Nonetheless, my satisfaction is legitimate, and the network has been able to satisfy my pride in a way that is completely automatic. The network is still full of surprises for us! And I believe that we will still see many fun things

Chapter 1
The internet revolution

Our world is in an advanced state of transformation between the reality that our parents and grandparents knew well and a new universe that is catching on faster and faster and that connects the real world more closely with the virtual world.

1.1 The birth of the internet

I was in high school when we began to tackle the topic of the internet and HTML, a language that allowed us to connect different documents to one another through hyperlinks, but above all to tie documents belonging to different computers to a large world network, the World Wide Web. It is strange to think how a trick of programming or a string more intelligent than the others can sometimes lead to epochal changes in the way of thinking and being of a company, willy-nilly, the internet has been able to completely revolutionize our way of thinking, buying products and services, getting to know people, falling in love with a person, caring for and following care plans and, as far as this book is concerned, also our way of doing business.

☐

Although the protocols for creating the internet had already been created in the 70s of the last century (ARPANET protocol), the World Wide Web as we know it was introduced in 1991 by Tim Berners-Lee, who was interested in creating a network to easily share documents among researchers at CERN in Geneva, where he worked. He was responsible for the development of the HTTP (Hypertext Transfer Protocol), characters that we still type today to reach a web page. It was then decided not to patent the protocol, and this allowed the immediate, exponential spread of the internet. Tracing the history of the internet is also a way of understanding how related both our society and the technological evolution are.

1.2 What can we do online today?

A few decades have passed, and if we tried to take stock of the last few years today, we could say that the online world has slowly but surely grown and developed. A decisive step, with the advent of iPhones, Tablets, and Smartphones, was to propagate network services directly at our fingertips, effectively sanctioning the birth of augmented reality just a click or voice command away.

Today we have a device at our disposal that allows us to be connected with the rest of the world at all times, not only to receive information but also to give it, even passively. When we are in traffic, for example, we are the ones who inform the satellites that follow us that queues are forming on that road. But we can also be proactive: we can upload a photo or video to a social network and write the review of a restaurant or hotel. It is also for this reason that the development of digital software and applications goes in the direction of simplification. From a Smartphone it is possible, for example, to take and edit the photo that was just taken with other tools at your fingertips, eliminating annoying imperfections such as red eyes and making sure that our skin has a more diffused shade and that wrinkles are reduced so that we can immediately share the photograph with a post. Through speech recognition, which is becoming more and more precise, we can convert our voice into a text that is pre-filled and orthographically correct, and therefore ready to be sent as an email or as a document. Simplification seems to be our new mantra, our new password, in a world where everything is in a hurry and every moment is useful for checking pending notifications, even waiting time. It could even seem that we are looking for empty moments, such as a trip on the subway or on a train, to carry on the work of constantly staying updated on the situations that regarding our life: our affections, our friends, politics, the weather, traffic, gossip ...

The reality around us is expanding and is continuously filled with supplementary pieces of information, some of which are of great use, whilst others turn out to be quite unnecessary. Today, we have no problem finding an address and following a navigator, we can book a table at a given restaurant or a night in a hotel with a single click or take a photo of a product that captures our attention to understand if it already exists on the internet, and hopefully its cost or how quickly they will deliver it to our home. We can learn from a great chef how to prepare a single dish step by step, or simply have it delivered to our home in a few minutes by one of the many delivery services we can choose. We can hop onto the car parked on our street -without being thieves! We'd just be using a car-sharing service and go where we want to, parking it somewhere else. This might look like the picture of a fantastic, unimaginable world which opens ever more unprecedented scenarios, but if we fail to manage these benefits in our business, we risk losing a great opportunity. Bigger groups already sign up and try to own rights on every activity that is simple to do to be the ones distributing these services and become industry leaders.

This is the reason why logistics, online research, e-mail and social networks already belong to a few large digital companies. But there is still a lot of room, we could even say it is infinite, given that the concepts of space and time are redefined on the internet, and therefore we can allocate space and time to talk about our peculiarities, to invest in our talent.

1.3 The origin of social networks

Several startups had begun to create communication and sharing channels between people who share interests already in the early 2000s. The first real social experiment with Myspace, a social that still exists de facto, was based on the world of artists. We had to wait until 2004 for Facebook to be born. The following year would see the birth of YouTube, a channel created to share videos; lately purchased by Google, it is one of the most viewed sites in the world that has also created a new professional figure: youtubers, who live off the proceeds of his/her videos. In the same years, a social network was going to transform the business world, becoming its reference channel. LinkedIn, now belonging to the Microsoft group, is probably the most valuable social network on the market. Finally, at the beginning of the first decade of this century, another social network based on sharing and correcting images acquired with smartphones and iPhones took hold: we're talking about Instagram, recently purchased by Facebook. We could say that social media have given new life to the internet by creating connections between people that are much stronger than connections between sites, to the point that today, for any professional or company, social media represents the starting point for lead generation activities. Chapter 4 will cover more details about this topic. Here, we will limit ourselves to say that our habit of using social media to share our information has allowed these platforms to have a huge amount of sensitive data available, from which targeted commercial campaigns can be built, i.e. aimed exactly at the audience that we want to influence. Thinking of sharing your resume with the whole world? Today you have LinkedIn. Have you ever imagined telling your mood to thousands of people with a post on Facebook, or sharing your family photo on Instagram? Later on, in this book we will learn to understand which social networks to use in order to find our customers and we will learn to redirect them to our blogs and web content. In some ways, the search engines and social networks, making a comparison with the real world, represent the streets, while the websites represent the shops, and the traffic is given by paid ads on social media (paid traffic). Unless our content goes viral: in that case, even if our shop is in the middle of the countryside, it will receive a substantial portion of traffic (organic traffic) completely for free. So the choice is yours!

1.4 The giants of the digital world

Addicted to everything for free and download just a click away, the global economic system has seen the appearance of huge players, who came into the game almost by chance: people with a long history behind them, myths and legends such as Bill Gates, Steve Jobs..., others passed to the fore in the most recent news; all these companies share a feature that is really important for our discussion: by simplifying user operations, constantly changing their algorithms, offering their services for free or with very competitive prices, they have gained powerful positions, both for the search for information and in the field entertainment and meetings on the net and the development and production of advanced digital solutions, voice recognition, sharing of experiences, development of immense databases, collection of information ...

Nowadays, we all have daily contact with these giants - Google, Amazon, Apple, and many others-, more or less. In our times their services are more used than the post office, their offers go beyond the borders of countries, replacing primary services that governments should perhaps offer. Today, a search starts from Google, a product is chosen on Amazon, a message is sent with WhatsApp because it guarantees us immediate confirmation of receipt, whilst in the past it was generally done with a registered e-mail with return receipt. But the world of millennials can no longer wait.

Nowadays, banks are online, stock market shares are bought in push mode, purchases are made by placing a credit card, or even better, by placing the smartphone near to a receiver, books are preferred in electronic format. Someone will object that reading a paper book is way more appealing, but everyone will agree that there is no faster way to get a book than to buy it in digital format.

And we are all sure that banknotes will disappear, and products will only be purchased online or with the functions of NFC. If you don't agree, let's talk about it again in a few years, when our children will ask us for our electronic pocket money and we will go shopping by showing our fingerprint, without any worries about leaving the wallet at home. The giants of the digital world are already thinking about all this, and dozens of new apps that are developed with the hope of simplifying a problem, solving a conflict, facilitating the provision of a service, are born every day.

This is the new world. How many years passed since we opened a dictionary for the last time? When did we calculate the result of a division as we learned in school, without the help of the specific calculating application on our smartphone? Today, the future is outlined by the developers of this parallel world, who are puzzling to reconstruct reality in a virtual way, so that a speech, a perfume, a transaction become a mathematical function like $y = f(x)$, ready to be sent to a satellite to continue jumping in the space and then be sent back to the sender whenever we wish to use it. At this point, perhaps, we should start to worry and begin to reflect on the fact that our life, the very essence of our existence, is reduced to a combination of mathematical functions that are able to describe our consumer profile in detail when grouped together. But it is useless to worry about our privacy only because we once looked for the photo of a sexy woman. In the end, none of the big giants cares about this so much. Rather, we can exploit all the information that we can easily find on the internet to our advantage, in our business.

We can use this information as metrics for our assessments. We can use the services to access a practically infinite audit of people, use the network to build our niche, the place on the market where our peculiarities, our skills, our sympathy, or perhaps even our flaws can become the opportunity to recruit more followers, to offer our products or services. This is a crucial step; no longer being in the position to be overwhelmed by technological progress, or losing our jobs because they have replaced us with a machine or an algorithm equipped with artificial intelligence, capable of doing our old job at a paltry cost and with an even lower error rate. We must somehow give up on pessimism and anticipate the future by dedicating ourselves to developing the applications that are certain to be necessary for the last generations; foreseeing a digital world in which we can work comfortably from home, without exhausting traffic jams and meetings with the office managers. We must, therefore, be able to become familiar with the services offered by the internet to use them to our advantage. To correctly calibrate our strategy, we must first submerge ourselves in our society, listen to the speeches of young people, understand how our children think, what they talk about, what they are interested in. Although they are a generation at risk, they are still the final recipients of the technological wonders that are offered to us every day. And they are the ones who teach their grandparents how to use the computer or smartphone. They are the digital natives, the generation of people able to handle tools that are not at all simple, with hidden keys, functions that are activated by placing three fingers of the right hand and two of the left hand simultaneously ("Dad was simple, it was enough to do so - my son would say - or you could watch the video tutorial on YouTube). And to them that is extremely easy!

First of all, let's try to understand what the mechanisms of our society are.

1.5 A liquid society

The last few decades have witnessed a radical change in our society, which we may not have been fully prepared for. Many of the cultural and historical structures have ceased to benefit a society that is perpetually connected and continually looking for new symbols and new myths. A fragile and constantly changing society, where age-old customs can be wiped out in a few handfuls of years. This constant instability created a strong sense of uncertainty, the frustrating feeling that nothing was stable. Today, the average life span of a company is less than fifteen years, while our working time becomes longer and longer. It is then clear then that we will not spend all our life in the same company but we will always be looking for new markets and new favorable economic conditions. Yet this reality, stigmatized by the philosopher and sociologist Zygmundy Baumann and perceived by him in a negative way, is the very structure of our society. What can we do to get a benefit? How can we go on with determining our target market and being profitable in this market segment? We can certainly build despite the general instability of the values that identify us on the market. How many times have we perceived the trust for a brand, perhaps when we found ourselves choosing between two similar garments, preferably the one whose brand expressed some values that mirrored our way of being more closely. Stability can arise from emotion but continues through the constancy that a product or service has.

We then choose the brand that is most similar to us, which best embodies our values and our vision of the world. Are we sporty, do we like challenges, travel, do we see the world in constant evolution? Are we open, eager to meet new people, to experience new? Are we constant, do we believe in the family, in traditional values? Every large company chooses its own archetypes and uses them in its own language with customers. The importance of this is clearly to induce a sense of stability. We feel protected, we feel reassured. Today, stability can be artificially induced by a fast food restaurant that offers its menu anywhere in the world, with the same taste. This is also a value, and in a society in constant evolution, a Big Mac will always have the same taste, unconditionally. So what can we do? We must determine what our values, our mission, even the colors that best represent us are, and use these values to build our identity, in such a way as to be uniquely recognized by our customers, and identified with our values in the language of our advertisements and our website and, more generally, in all our media exposure. Our consistency will be our strength in fighting a society that gradually loses its values.

1.6 Understanding human society before taking action

Before we even start our company, we should start worrying about being interpreters of our society. What is the risk otherwise? If we are unable to understand our society, we may not understand its needs and therefore risk not to have a market at all. But our society exists, it is connected, and buys. You read well, it also buys, for to exist and expand iit spends a lot of money. There is no shortage of money in this consumerist society, indeed, it has somehow been able to move economic value from physical, tangible goods to goods of a virtual nature. My nine-year-old son asked me to have a new skin of the current main character of his videogame. He insisted for several days. He promised me he would get a good grade at school. And when I finally bought it to him, he told me that that had been an extraordinary day for him. The sincerity of children is sometimes unsettling.

Once, you could choose a job based on your vocation and skills and everything would go smoothly. We were paid for the time we spent in our working place and since all - or almost all- work activities always waste time, we would come back home in the evening feeling as if our bones had broken, but always ready to start a new day. Then the internet came, and the world changed. Today, we can find our vocation just like yesterday, but we must go one step further, and study the market as well, where money flows towards. Why? First of all, because we want to be profitable, and then because the world is already giving us this information, and it would be stupid not to accept it. We must turn into experienced hackers and find the key to reach our customers, to know who they are, how much money they are willing to spend on a product similar to what we would like to sell them.

If we want to build profitable businesses, we have to understand our own society, what the newest trends, the desires and problems of people are. The advantage of the digital world is the ability to easily find information, to be able to find numbers, and numbers tell us how much interest there is in a product or service. We somehow take advantage of this additional information. when in possession of it, we must become aware of both what we know how to do and what we love to do, and these are things that belong to us, to our sphere of competence, our personality. But the digital world gives us two other aspects that are fundamental to finding our ikigai, that is, we have the tools to understand what society actually needs, and what people are willing to spend their money on and pay to get that thing. Only then will we find our ikigai: the love for what we like to do, combined with our skills, will make us live our work experience with passion, and the fact of knowing that we are working for a good cause will make us perceive this as a mission. But that's also what a non-profit organization can do. To be profitable, we must get to the market, we must become aware that money can transform our passion into a profession and the satisfaction of a need in a vocation.

The strength of this scheme is such as to keep us strong even in difficult moments. If we only worked for money and, in a time of crisis, even money disappeared, how could we be rewarded? Instead, many times we might have heard people say that even if they were not making money at the time, they were passionately carrying out their mission, and better times would come, anyway!

1.7 From scratch to enterprise with digital tools

Initially, digital technology seemed to simplify some aspects of our lives. Discs were no longer vinyl, but had become compact disks, with the advantage of hosting multiple tracks; the photographic film was no longer needed to take pictures, since the photos were immediately recorded on the sensor, with the advantage of being able to check them immediately on the screen and to intervene in time, if the taken picture was blurred. Then, the transformation of analog information into digital information slowly began to bring about epochal changes that would shortly transform society as well. Music was moved from CDs to the internet, and as a consequence, it could follow us everywhere. The concept of ownership of an asset also changed, as it is now linked to technological support and time of sharing, not the possession of an asset. Material support, essentially, dematerialized. The photographs themselves were immediately available to be shared on social networks, without needing to be printed, but directly usable on smartphones and tablets. Not only that, but it was also no longer necessary to organize an exhibition and invite our friends to admire them, as they could already be seen and commented on by millions of people on the net. Indeed, photographs became functional to describe a place to a person who does not know it.

The world has had us grow accustomed to so many small digital aids that have become an integral part of our new era. Many digital giants have paved the way for us, providing us with extremely advanced tools at zero cost or at very reduced costs. Now, we must learn to use these very tools to our advantage. For example, until a few years ago if we had wanted to set up a company, we would have thought of looking for an apartment, providing it with landlines, secretaries, accounting, commercial office, order office, warehouse. Today, many of these functions can be entrusted to a web algorithm or an app on our smartphone.

This book aims to learn how to manage a company by trying to exploit all the digital resources available today. So, in the next chapters, we will learn to see step by step how we could manage our digital content and be able to create an adequate structure to develop profitable businesses with extremely reduced costs. For us, the opportunity to save on activation costs may as well be the chance to always test new business models and understand what profitable trends are. We will start by learning what these trends are using Google's search tools, then we will discover how social media represent formidable advertising platforms for leads generation. We will land on our landing page that we will have learned to build with WordPress, and finally we will learn to build our digital funnel and to manage our digital content effectively and profitably to create value around our proposal. Now the choice remains how quickly we want to grow!

1.8 To grow slowly, or to become a unicorn?

Now, the question is: how to take advantage of the advances that were made possible by the digital world to make sure our company will grow? And how quickly should this company grow, based on the value we are transmitting? We should think in terms of virality. Nowadays, these concepts have become sadly famous because of the coronavirus pandemic, but if we talk about the aspect of the spread only, we can think that speed, in case of growth, is one of the concepts that could guide us in the distribution of our value. Today, in fact, it is not a problem to reach the whole world with the message I want to send, just like it was not difficult for a tiny virus to tilt all the world continents with the exception of Antarctica. The problem is mainly about our proposal and the value associated with it, and about scalability.

These aspects are important, especially when we want to think in terms of growth in an ecosystem that is generally hostile to it. For example, if we want to open an e-commerce, even though, from a digital point of view, it is easy to retrieve all the elements to build one that is formally complete, elegant, and graphically cute, we know very well that we will go up against giants like Amazon, who own enormous power capable of annihilating us in a moment. We must always be aware of this when we want to do great things. I recently attended an academy to focus on staff training and the creation of businesses. A boy came up to me, wanting to talk about his project, which he considered particularly interesting, so much he wished to realize it at all costs. I saw that he couldn't hide his excitement while thinking about his idea, but at the same time, he didn't want to share it with many people for he feared that someone could steal it. However, he began to speak and told me that he wanted to create something that would be halfway between Facebook and Amazon and that it would change the way we buy and share information. I understood that he was very euphoric, and as soon as he could, he took part in the conversation with the organizers who also astounded themselves as they advised him to reflect more calmly on that idea and to avoid exposing himself financially.

More generally, most entrepreneurs say they need money to build a prototype and demonstrate to the world that their idea is fantastic. They assume that growth should not be demonstrated for a new startup. This is definitely wrong, and to be honest, it is a typical problem of mediocre founders, guided by the desire to build what they want and love, rather than finding a solution to a problem of their own clients. After spending years asking for funding and seeing that their idea does not work, instead of failing quickly, and starting again with a new project closer to the real needs of the people, what do they do? They try to add features to their idea and turn it into a monster with many heads. Clearly, none of us are able to build something like Microsoft or Apple overnight, and their idea can only miserably fail, after many years of fruitless attempts to keep it alive. Instead, good entrepreneurs focus on one aspect and try to build an ecosystem of products and services that becomes functional in solving the problem they have identified. Even big projects like Instagram were born as simplification, not a complication. Kevin Systrom worked on an app with the name of difficult pronunciation,

Burbn, a location and sharing service that was quite dispersive. However, there was a part of it widely used by users that allowed you to share photos and use filters effectively. At that point, Kevin decided to focus only on that part and create Instagram. This proves simplifying things is way better than complicating them; what allows us to achieve success in the digital world is the accuracy of our digital marketing content, rather than in the mix of confused ideas,

1.9 Is the Internet empty?

Working in digital marketing, I always wondered if the internet was a huge empty box or vice versa, a place for meeting, exchanging, information, sharing. This doubt of mine arose from the fact that in the beginning, very few people used the internet to share value. We talk about value when we want to express something that is important to me. But what is value and how can it be transmitted through a cold machine, like a digital tool? Value is something that makes our heart beat faster, which gives us emotions. It is clear that these types of values mainly belong to the real world, not to the digital one. But if you think about it, after all, it's just a matter of habit. For example, cinema has made it possible to transmit very intense emotions through an means that has not always existed. For the Internet, the problem is even more delicate because, as we have seen, the birth of the Internet was essentially due to the rapid sharing of documents and the rapid exchange of information. The immense web space that was being created over the years was essentially a showcase for some companies. Then came the interactive applications, which implemented JAVA software packages capable of animating web pages. Today a website can act as a telephone, television, a chat for eroticism and sexuality, a way to transmit information, distribute books, sell services and products, and we could say that there are almost no limits to the things that can be done through the internet. Gradually, we began to feel emotions, to return to a web page to read information, to constantly use that online service just because it simplifies our life. Hence, even though we often browse sites that have no value, which are only advertising or replicating other sites, there is also a slight chance that there are sites and services that contain a lot of value, at least for us, like other things we do in life. But to go back to our paradox, is the internet full or empty? Are our contents visible or hidden?

To answer this question, we must consider the search engines and social media that have made it possible to reach web content. Our content will be found and our pages will be populated by users, but only if we establish a strategy to drive traffic to our valuable content. Now we will learn how to do it!

Chapter 2

Increase our reality

In this chapter, we will explore different areas of the digital world and try to find ideas to better understand our reality and to think about how we can still find profitable markets in this world in continuous transformation.

2.1 Being connected to the new world

It seems strange to think that even unwittingly, the augmented world has become a powerful part of our daily lives. As proof of this I can tell two anecdotes that demonstrate how both the old generations and the new ones have entered the digital world to a large extent, and we, who represent the intermediate generation, and have how it was to live in the old world, one made of concrete stuff like trees, but are now constantly struggling with smartphones and tablets, can try to take stock of this transformation. As proof of the inevitability of the digital world and the transformations we have undergone because of the liquid society and the market. I'll do this comparing two generations. that of my almost ninety-year-old father and that of my son, who recently turned eight.

I recently followed some seminars on economic transformations and during a presentation of business models and new economics the speaker explained that the smartphones we all own did not buy them for our choice, but for an imposition of the market. The reasoning was absolutely logical, but I could not fully understand the link, the truest meaning. I was thinking, for example, of my parents who have old generation mobile phones. Once back home, my mom called me all out of breath and asked me to join my father in his room because for some days he had been unable to access his bank account via internet. In fact, his bank has decided to eliminate the token, a device that generates access numbers to the bank's portal, and asks its customers to download the app from their smartphone. My father had spoken several times with the bank's technical assistance, without being able to solve the problem. When I calmly explained to him what the problem was, my laconic father said he would rush to buy a smartphone. Just at that moment, the words of the speaker came back to me: we did not choose this technology, but it was our economy that imposed it on us.

Just in these days, some friends have invited our child to play with other children. We were happy that our son could socialize with other kids by spending Sunday afternoons together. We, adults, were chatting, and the kids had gone downstairs to the playroom. When we went down to see what they were doing, there were a dozen children between 8 and 11 years old, everyone was playing with their smartphone. Somewhat annoyed, I then asked my son why he had taken my smartphone and why they were playing on their own. My son replied: "dad, we are all playing together with Brawl Stars, we are all connected here!". I didn't say anything else and went back upstairs to chat with the other parents.

2.2 Homo Sapiens and Homo Digitalis

The boundaries between the real world and the virtual one are getting smaller and smaller. Information technology, network capability and artificial intelligence, in addition to the power and stability of the internet, are the pillars of the new digital world and the changes will not only be continuous but also incredible if we also consider that the ability of machines to learn behavior starting from the statistical data collected automatically on the behavior of people, and finally, the ability that IT has to store information and make it available in an increasingly simple way wherever we are. A world of commodities that will characterize our future is already being built on these pillars. At this moment we are in full transformation, and we have already noticed that a competition of giants has started to grab the essential digital structures, the information highways. But we are still in time to take advantage of this revolution, be the restaurant near the highway junction, which collects part of the highway traffic. But apart from this metaphor, knowing how to manage digital tools means being able to reap the benefits, to hack the systems the giants can't or are not interested in getting to, and those niches could be useful for our business.

But let's see what is happening to our world. A particularly insidious virus has caused almost all the nations to go into lockdown, it has filled the hospitals with patients and put several productive sectors into crisis. Many, but not all. Before the lockdown, a few years ago, I had convinced myself that Homo Sapiens was slowly giving way to Homo digitalis. Homo Sapiens thrives on physical, concrete relationships. He works in companies, has shops, industries and he produces manufactured, quality goods or fashionable clothes. Homo Sapiens travels tens of thousands of miles every year on the highway and preferentially uses the mobile phone to communicate, he is pragmatic, sometimes short-tempered, generally brilliant, attentive to his behavior and how he communicates. He is the alpha male of the species. And until now, he had no doubts about his resistance. But the world was already changing: those who decided to go online found themselves saving time on the move, building lifestyles more suited to their spontaneity, sleeping peacefully at home and already looking at their results on the dashboard in the morning. Then coronavirus came and subverted every law of the world. The elegant man in the car of his company, the man in pajamas with a cup of coffee in his hand and comfortable slippers... Suddenly, a microscopic virus changed the rules of the game and allowed a new species, perhaps less strong and aggressive, less brilliant, to be successful, for a period, to continue its online business undisturbed and to keep invoicing never putting his health at risk. This species was lazy to the point of having his shopping brought home with a click of the mouse, taking advantage of the virtual discount coupons he had previously accumulated.

Homo digitalis has more time to read, to study, and his attention is caught by many different things every day; he can stay updated on historical events, strings of commands, procedures for building an online funnel. This sly gentleman, with his comfortable suit and slippers, is not very sociable or familiar with phones, and even less with direct relationships with people. But he has a great ability to write emails, tell interesting stories, or to find attractive pictures to create an advertising banner. If he has already saved some money, he can start an online campaign and launch the e-commerce of a friend who produces jams from chestnuts in the woods around his home or import led bulbs from China and sell them at three times their price, all of this without having a warehouse and only by uploading the technical data sheet and a photograph of the product on a site. Homo digitalis is shyer than homo sapiens but has many stories to tell and very broad culture. He can switch from one speech topic to another with virtuous connections, and he's not

39

monothematic like the Sapiens seller. If the LED bulbs business doesn't go to breakeven, or the e-commerce page does not take off, he will not stress over it that much: instead, he'll register the loss of a few hundred euros and decide to devote himself to online clothing for jockeys, a niche that now seems profitable to him. Should his new sportswear e-commerce work well, he'll decide to expand to the golf clothing field too; he is still single but has a bicycle and tools at home, and now he would like to get involved. He is not as fascinating as homo sapiens, who had a good chance of success when preying on a potential partner. Homo digitalis would not be able to compete in direct competition. For this, he will just open an application, browse some girls the server selected based on similar interests and habits -there are thousands of them in the database- and in the end, he'll find love matches on the other side of the ocean. "Who's going to visit the other, me or you?" After a few months, he'll be the one leaving his house, renting it and moving to his new girlfriend's. What about his job? Of course, it'll go on as always, without interruption. Homo digitalis is no longer strong, but he is more able to adapt to the environment and he can reproduce without a problem. This is why we think that homo digitalis will in the long run be the only one that will survive.

2.3 To be retargeted in a replica reality

The virtual world is entering the real one more and more; there is an interpenetration of the two worlds that has accelerated drastically from the widespread diffusion of smartphones, that have become our main prosthesis. Smartphones have learned to know us better, to understand our habits, to advise us based on our preferences. Among the worst aspects of this pursuit, retargeting is one of those aspects that should probably be regulated the most, but if used correctly, it can be an effective way of putting the buyer in contact with us.

However, is the perception of reality really honest, or do we suffer a cognitive bias? Suppose that you have to change your car and that you have been very clear about the fact that the new car you want must be red. Suddenly, looking around on the net, you'll see red cars everywhere. Now let's imagine we have searched for a new washing machine on our favorite e-commerce. From that moment, washing machines will appear around us on every banner and every website. Should we show interest in digital content management, on Facebook, every three posts we'll find anew guru who offers his digital content management course. An inattentive eye might think that everyone wants to buy that course. In reality, it is us who have influenced the algorithms of social networks, and we are continually brought back to the same reality. The digital world is somewhat more insidious: it tends to accommodate reality to our values, our interests, our favorite brands, leading us to become the creators of hybrid reality, so we will fail to discern what really happens from what happens because we built it ourselves in our virtual paths.

2.4 The plant kingdom, the internet and the blockchain

When we think of artificial intelligence and robotics, the first idea that comes to mind is that of Hal, the "Space Odyssey" robot. Even if we think of a computer and break it down into its parts, it essentially resembles a humanoid: the processor, which represents a synthetic version of the brain; then the memory, which is closely connected with the processor, and then cascades all the other peripherals; the video card, which could be imagined as our ability to see and manage images; the sound card, our ability to listen and reproduce sounds; the printer, which is the hard copy of our activities, just as we make drawings, or write in a notebook. Similarly, when we think of a robot, we imagine it with anthropomorphic characteristics, its head, its motor apparatus and arms, and its ability to orient itself. However, there is another type of robotic intelligence that we know well but that does not immediately come to mind. We are talking about the internet, which, especially starting from the era of smartphones, represents a widespread intelligence that communicates with us, learns from our behavior. The Internet is stable because it is a network made up of many hubs and many connections, most of which are delocalized, not centralized, therefore the possible blackout of one of these hubs does not determine the instability of the entire network. A widespread encyclopedia has also been developed, where anyone with the appropriate skills can add content, a traffic forecasting service based on the data of the users themselves, therefore with interactive feedback. A network, in some ways similar to the network of plants, a fixed but absolutely dynamic network, where all of us are connected and receive information that allows us to survive if managed well, where we can interact, and even facilitate mating.

Recent experiments have led to understanding that plants have adaptability, memory, and survival skills that we had not yet suspected so far. For example, an experiment was carried out on two different samples. The former was subjected to a water reduction, the latter was not. Then, both specimens were re-hydrated for a few months, and later, both had to undergo a reduction of water. It has been seen that the one who had already experienced dehydration reacted to stress better. This has opened up a field of studies aimed at demonstrating the existence of epigenetic foundations, for which plants have memory. But as we know, plants don't have a brain. Hence, within them, the management of memory is distributed in cells and delocalized. NASA is carrying out experiments with plantoids, robots that emulate the shape and behavior of plants and may be the first intelligent beings to populate the surface of Mars, to create the environmental conditions for human colonization.

Still, in the relocation logic, a structure similar to that of plants is one that offers greater stability. An example of all is the blockchain, a widespread and shared database that becomes stable and protected by virtue of its relocation to the point that it can be used to manage protected information. The blockchain represents a chain of blocks and is a shared and immutable structure, whose integrity is guaranteed by cryptography. Once again, relocation guarantees stability and security. Blockchain is an emerging sector for those wishing to develop innovative businesses for the secure management of information. Why are stability and encryption so important? The reason why they count so much is that if you have the certainty of an event, or the registration of a transaction, without the need of an intermediary (for example the bank) that guarantees its validity, you can imagine many consequences in applications and services. To create currencies without needing a bank, for example, or to trace the production chain of a certified product; to fight crime and illegality; for the validation of documents. Where could the IT infrastructure bring great progress? Probably in the strategic use of Blockchain, Information Technology, and the Internet of Things. Why? Let's try to clarify. The fact that today more and more tools, such as TVs, washing machines, ovens, lighting systems, etc., are connected to the internet, allows you to use the IT infrastructure to manage them.

We could easily imagine a future in which many of the routine functions of our daily lives are performed by smart appliances with robotic capabilities. But how can we be sure then that the operations will be carried out with certainty? Who can assure us that automatic transactions will be tracked? Blockchain is an incorruptible database, a register that doesn't need an intermediary to register with due certainty that an operation or a task has been carried out, and, therefore, that an economic transaction can take place. Let's think, for example, of electricity or gas meters. Or think of self-driving cars that will have to document a possible accident. In this way, no human being will have to perform mere control operations, but all these functions will be automated and updated on our database, without possible tampering. The future is only at the beginning and those who try their hand at these entrepreneurial activities will be able to write the pages of this story.

2.5 Internet Technology, Artificial Intelligence and Machine Learning

Why are we inclined to believe that this fast growth of the digital and IT world is destined to continue? You have probably heard of Artificial Intelligence (AI) and Machine Learning. These concepts are the theoretical foundations of a world in which a whole series of skills that are simple for a computer to perform is delegated to the machine. In general, the computer is a machine capable of doing simple but repetitive things. For example, an ATM has replaced an employee serving in a bank, a boring and repetitive job, and this was possible with little added value that made it possible for that person to be replaced by a machine in all of their tasks. More generally, we must get used to thinking that man is gradually implementing a new industrialization process, which is to understand the behavior of people and learn from them. For example, imagine you are entering a fashion store; you ask the clerk what clothes are in fashion at that moment, or maybe the one showcasing the most current fashion items is exactly the clerk. Now suppose, instead, to be visiting an e-commerce site built in such a way as to be able to experience the same emotions, to perceive what is actually going out of fashion. In particular, trendy items are exhibited in a virtual showcase, but that this virtual showcase updates itself based on actual purchases, or the needs of the warehouse. If people search the site fora piece of clothing that is not on the front page, the algorithm that manages the virtual shop window memorizes the customer's behavior, and consequently alters the shop window, highlighting the clothes that they're selling the most at the moment.

Here, we are explaining in simple words the meaning of artificial intelligence, i.e. an algorithm capable in this case of modeling itself on the propensity to purchase customers. At this point, the same algorithm could automatically update the window and redefine prices, to see if customers are still willing to buy despite the slight increase. In this way, our e-commerce is not only a passive IT box programmed to repeat the same things over and over, but it is trained to act as both a salesperson and a sales manager and is autonomously able to take initiative based on the behavior of sale. Thanks to increasingly effective programming levels and the ability to use the analytical results of some information, such as sales data, to automatically modify others -for example, which articles to highlight and at what cost- we are faced with processed, sophisticated shop management. Now imagine introducing other variables, such as the automatic counting of the stock, and the request to increase the production of the most requested garments: all this allows us to have completely automatic production processes. In the near future, we can expect further steps forward in artificial intelligence. For now, let's just observe that design, creativity, the ability to put together different concepts and find innovative solutions to old problems are typical skills of our brain, and those for the moment will be difficult to achieve with automatic algorithms. At least right now.

2.6 The innovation of Living Books Insights

In my life, I have read many books, both fiction and non-fiction ones. Many of them helped me grow immediately, while others passed quickly, but they still left me with some ideas that cemented together with my training and made me grow anyway. On the other hand, there are books to which I am very fond, which have somehow continued to play a role in my life, as if they were still alive and I could still take something from that inexhaustible source of experience. Novels, as they are conceived, especially those written by good novelists, do not end with a "happily ever after". A good storyteller knows how to leave room for the reader's imagination. In fact, I could say, I don't like books where you can feel that "everything is clear" in the end. Books of which you only understand a part, even a good one, but that leave you with questions that in the following days, months, or years, will continue to remain unanswered by the author, gradually come to our imagination and give us feedback. For a novel, in general, it is not a great idea to know how the story ends in detail unless it is a serial novel: stories continue in our heads, and they'll be recreated continuously. Conversely, when we read a book about a specific topic we would like to mark those references, those procedures which then come in hand in everyday life. Here, instead, we want to continue updating online content and receive constant updates, links to websites of interest, some interactive examples of configuring a CMS, and interactive space. In this way, books continue to exist and are useful even after reading is finished. Also this possibility, like many others described in this book, is made possible by our ally, the web, a platform that allows us to do many things as well as to report useful links and tutorials and allow us to find them easily wherever we are. If you find that the topics covered in this book are interesting for you, feel free to keep living this experience and enjoying its utility online, so that, in the digital age, even a book can have, a different shape, a continuous updating, a dynamic becoming.

Chapter 3

The Google Galaxy

3.1 Social Media Marketing

As the global marketing industry is ever-evolving, it is essential to stay up to date with trends and concepts that will keep you fresh in the marketplace. This includes knowing where people are living a great deal of their life. The trends have moved from traditional marketing channels to that of a digital world. It seems as though the amount of individuals using social networks is still increasing. Along with that, the time they spend on these social networks has become where they are digitally living. This means businesses need to understand how to tap into the digital lifestyle.

In the next pages, you will learn some basics about google and how it can benefit your business, a brief of some of the most popular social networks and emerging networks, and how to manage collected data from these places and make it work for your business.

Choices are abundant when it comes to an understanding of social media marketing, and choosing this book was a great start. A heartfelt and genuine thank you for your purchase. I made every effort to pull together a quick and easy to read guide for you to grow your social media marketing. So let's get started!

Driving traffic to your business or website is a necessity to grow yourself in the digital world. However, it recognizes the difference between social marketing and search engine marketing and how they can work together. These are both primary marketing techniques that businesses can use to drive their online presence. However, it often is a struggle to decide which is the best way to invest those precious marketing funds.

Think of yourself for a moment and when you are looking for a business. Do you use a search to find them? A report found that 61% of consumers use a search engine like google before making a purchase. The thing that is important to understand is both of these matters.

3.2 Google Search

Let's talk about why search is important to think about the ways that you look for a product or service in your area. More and more people go to their good friend google and start their search. It has become a habit and one that people of all ages are using to get the results they are looking for. If you were looking for a Zumba instructor in your area, it is ten times more likely that you would go to your favorite search engine (google ranking in at the top) and search for Zumba Instructors in your area.

Many tools are available for marketing when it comes to google one key tool is Google Keywords Planner, which I will touch a bit more on later. When we think of marketing to rank high through organic means, we are looking at the search engine optimization (SEO) for your site. Keyword research fits more than just with your website; it also transitions to your social media platforms. Within Google Ads software, they also have a build it keywords tool. This can prove to be very helpful. It can help you see the difference in one term versus another. So a pet store might use pet supplies rather than pet supply and have a significantly higher ranking in search.

So how do you get your ranking higher organically? Well, it goes back to your SEO; when your website is optimized for users and search engines, you push yourself further up the algorithm. Some common practices for SEO are keywords, URLs, content, and optimizing title tags.

Google uses an algorithm analyzer to crawl websites for keywords; it's a very smart process and looks for specific keywords on your page. If those keywords appear on the page or in the body or heading of the text, your site is seen as more relevant. But there is more to it than just simply filling your site with keywords. It also checks your site for user experience, bounce rate, search intent, loading speed, and click-through-rate.

So let's talk first a little more about keywords. In the first 100 -150 words of your article, it is very important to use your main keyword at least once. So if my blog or post were optimizing the keyword "social marketing," I would mention that word straight away. Possibly in the heading or the first sentence. This is because Google puts more weight on terms that show up early in on the page or post. This is a pretty basic concept since you would typically do this in your post to begin with. You wouldn't wait until halfway down the page to start talking about social marketing if your post or page were about that.

So this is why you want to drop the majority of your keywords somewhere in the first 100 words. It is just one of those little ideas that will help Google algorithm understand what your page or post is about. The frequency of your keywords is also a factor when it comes to your ranking. SEO pros always suggest that the use of the same keywords multiple times builds your page's topic structure and clarifies to the algorithm that what the page is about.

So let's talk optimizing content tags. Using H1 tags is another important part of your post or page. This helps not only your user understand the structure of the page, but it also helps Google's fancy algorithm to understand the structure. Many sites already have this built-in if you are using a WordPress platform or something similar you should be able to automatically see that it is creating an H1 tag to the title of your post. However, if you are unsure, you can always check with the person who programmed your site to ensure that it is using H1 tags.

Often underrated is the stricter of your URL for SEO. The key things here are to make your URLs short and include keywords in every URL. I love this part because it's not complicated, super straight forward and easy. It is okay to have other words rather than your keyword in the URL as well; it is also okay to have the keyword follow the subfolder.

We could really talk about SEO and how it optimization of it can boost your website further, but these are honestly the best places to get started and begin to crush it with google. The next two sections are going to focus more on tools you have to use with google to help drive your marketing strategy trends and Google Ads.

3.3 Google Trends

Google is such a powerful tool to have in your mix as a marketer. It has so many different features built-in that can help you to dive in and make educated business decisions. For this section, we are going to take a look at Google Trends, another tool Google has provided for businesses to see the popularity of a term and the popularity of the term by region over a specific period. If you are just starting in marketing, this tool can be a lifesaver. You will be able to use it to help to research keywords and discover valuable insight around those keywords. It can allow you to look at keywords and target people that may not be already using your products. Let's say you are launching a Superhero Pet line. Your typical keywords would not necessarily target those interested in superheroes. Yet, with the research, you could find the optimized target words to drive new customers to your site. Another amazing thing about Google Trends is it is free to use. You simply just visit

3.4 Google Ads

Our next topic is Google Ads, which is an online advertising solution from Google to help business promote their goods and services within Google Search YouTube and across other sites as well. The solution allows the advertiser to set their own goals and desired outcomes. If you want to drive people to your site or to call you, then you can set those targets up. If you are looking to target a budget or specific segment group, then you can do that as well. Another beautiful thing about Google ads is you can stop an ad at any time.

So remember earlier, we were talking about using SEO to rank in search results organically? Well, Google Ads is another way to pay for your ranking. It works by displaying your ad when people search for services or products you offer. It uses a smart system of technology to help you get your ads in front of prospective customers at the moment when they are ready to take action.

To begin setting up your Ads, you would start by selecting a goal this could be increasing the number of visitors to your site or increasing the number of calls to your business. Then you would select the geographic area you would like your ad to be shown. It can be as small as your local city or as broad as the entire world. It is what you want to set it. The final step is crafting your ad and applying your desired budget cap. Once all of these things are completed, your add will then be sent to Google for approval. Once approved, it will appear wherever your target audience is, and you will only pay when users engage with it by clicking or calling your business.

The next most common thing that people want to understand more is how much this cost will. The honest answer is it depends on your keywords and where they are ranking. If you pick a word that ranks really high, then it is likely that you will need a bigger budget to meet more people. Google Ads does have a few different ways that you can pay for advertising. They offer Cost Per Click (CPC) or Pay Per Click (PPC); this basically means that when the ad is clicked on, you pay. The other advertising models they have are Cost Per Impression, which is where you pay depending on how many times your ad is shown not clicked. The last way is the cost per engagement, and this is typically seen more with video, where you pay when a user completes a predefined engagement like a poll or watching a video. With all of this said, it is recommended that you spend about 30 minutes a week following up with your ad results and reviewing any adjustments you need to make for the campaign. One great thing is that Google Ads has an app for both Android and iOS so you can actually make changes and adjustments on the go.

One thing to remember is you are learning, and it might take time for you to experience success with your campaigns. It is not likely that you will see success overnight. On average, it takes approximately 30 days to see results from your ads. So when planning your budget, make sure that you consider this.

One really cool thing is getting started with Google Ads is free. There is not a fee to create a Google Ads account, and you can start right away by signing up at https://ads.google.com . Google even offers a guided step by step setup processes to help you create your first ad and get you rolling. If you are still struggling or have questioned Google, has a team of Ads experts available to help you set your new account up or even assist in creating your campaign at no additional cost. So why not put them to work for you and learn from the pros?

3.5 Google Keyword Planner

It would be remiss of me not to talk about Google Keyword planner. This is a tool that you can use overall social networks and your website. It can help you to grow organic traffic that costs you nothing. As well it can also help you when you are spending those precious marketing budget dollars.

To access the Google Keyword Planner, which is a free tool! You simply will log into your Google Ads account. If you do not have one go ahead and set up a Google Ads account.

https://ads.google.com/home/

It is really quite simple to set up; you just follow the prompts, and before you know it, you have your account set up and linked to your business. Then you will need to log into your Google Ads Account.

Then you will choose under planning Keyword Planner.

These tools are very powerful and have the potential to generate thousands of possible keywords literally for you as they were designed for those looking for PPC advertisers. Yet, just because that is what they were designed for does not mean that this is the only way you can use this information. This is where you can dive into and see where some words are going to have a higher PPC price than others. However, these same words can be used as part of your SEO or as hashtags on your social media to drive higher in the fancy google algorithm.

For this example, let's just look at simply "Discover new keywords" much as the name suggests; it is a tool for finding keywords. When you click that box, another box will pop up. As seen below, you will see that it asks you to enter services or products that relate to your business. This is where it is essential to be strategic in what you put in this field. So as you can see from the graphic below, you will have a couple of different options for looking for keywords you can enter specific words that closely relate to your service or business, or you can start with a website.

If you choose to start with a website, you will just simply drop your domain name in there, and it will generate keywords based on what it sees on that page or site. If you are specifically looking to drive customers to one product, be sure to use that specific page URL.

However, we recommend using words that relate to your business to drive a greater amount of potential keywords. So begin by thinking of a few keywords, let's use the example of a coffee store. So you might include keywords of decaf, coffee, or cold brew. As you enter each word or grouping of words, hit the enter key to turn it to the dark blue color.

Once you have your keywords all entered, you will then simply click Get Results. Google will begin generating a list of keywords that align with your search results. Regardless of what way you decide to search for keywords, it will lead you to a search result page similar to what I have below. Now keep in mind that your keywords may not be the same from specific words you picked and the page you told it to use. It is always great to run the search on both and see what differences you can come across and broaden your keywords.

Keyword (by relevance) ↓	Avg. monthly searches	Competition
Keywords you provided		
☐ decaf	1K – 10K	Low
☐ coffee	1M – 10M	Low
☐ cold brew	10K – 100K	High
Keyword ideas		
☐ coffee near me	100K – 1M	Low
☐ best coffee near me	100K – 1M	Low
☐ cafe near me	100K – 1M	Low
☐ cappuccino	100K – 1M	Medium
☐ coffee shops near me	100K – 1M	Low
☐ espresso	10K – 100K	High
☐ barista	10K – 100K	Low
☐ latte	10K – 100K	Low
☐ bulletproof coffee	100K – 1M	High

So what we can see here is how these words rank on google. This will help you find the best words for you. The Avg. monthly searches is a great column to look at on this form as it gives you insight as to how frequently these terms are searched. This allows you to be really competitive in terms of what is on-trend, by clicking on the words Avg. Monthly searches, you can sort the list by lowest to highest or highest to lowest searches. Now both of these are important; obviously, the words being searched the most are ones that you should be using in your SEO or hashtags. However, the ones not being searched quite as much should be words you are avoiding.

The next column is the competition; this one is tricky for many and trips up new marketers quite often. The competition score here only refers to competition on AdWords, not how competitive the keyword is in ranking for Google. This is useful to know when creating google ads because of the higher the competition, the greater amount you potentially will pay for that word.

Which brings us to the next part of the keywords report, now this will only be useful for those choosing to run Google ads if the next important column is the top of page bid (low range) and then the top of page bid (high range).

Keyword	Avg. monthly searches	Competition ↓	Ad impression share	Top of page bid (low range)	Top of page bid (high range)
Keywords you provided					
cold brew	10K – 100K	High	–	$0.79	$4.38
Keyword ideas					
french press	100K – 1M	High	–	$0.18	$0.55
nespresso pods	10K – 100K	High	–	$1.54	$31.32
aeropress	10K – 100K	High	–	$0.53	$1.29

We can see that cold brew was one of our keywords with high competition, and the low range bid starts at $0.79 per click and the high range top of page bid starts at $4.38 per click when we look at that same information for one of the suggested keywords Nespresso pods we see that the low range is $1.54 and the high is $31.32. This simply means that the person who is getting that top spot for the keyword searched "Nespresso pods" is paying a potential $31.32 to show up in that top spot. I say potential because it is all about bidding; this $31.32 can be pushed up by someone else bidding $31.10 for the number two spot. When you set your keywords, you will be able to set your max bid for your ads to help you maintain your budget. This is also why it is not something you can set it and forget it. You need to actively manage your Google Ads to ensure that you are getting the best bang for your buck. In contrast, you may look at the competition that is at a medium level for your google ads and still use "Nespresso pods" on your site to drive your organic search results rather than paying for the top spot.

The biggest thing to remember when using the Google Keyword Tool is you are looking for keywords that will help to drive people to you. How you do that might look different from platform to platform. The best thing about Google, however, is that all of these services and products are free for you to work towards driving your marketing to the next level.

For a step by step tutorial of the procedures adopted here and in next chapters, you will benefit from a clickable version of these pages with more examples and useful links in the living page of this book at:

https://www.lineprofile.net/digital-content

where you will find also additional materials related to the next chapters.

Chapter 4

Socially useful Networks

Connections are truly what matters when it comes to social media marketing regardless of what social network you are using. When first starting out, you might be tempted to jump into all social networks and learn everything. However, this may not be the best approach; sometimes, it is better to be great at one thing first before you branch out into other areas. Only you know yourself and what you are capable of. At the end of the day, the goal is to grow your network and connect with your customers or clients.

4.1 Facebook

Connecting is important, no matter which network you choose. Facebook has designed its algorithm around this specifically. There are 2.5 billion individuals who use Facebook to connect with family, friends, and discover what is important to them. As a business, it is important to build upon those relationships, especially for small and medium-sized businesses with tight budgets. Facebook is designed to help businesses of all sizes and skill levels to accomplish business goals. It is quite obvious in today's economy that no two businesses are quite the same. This is where the beauty of where the connection comes to play. Through Facebook, a business is able to tell their story in a way that is meaningful to their customers or potential customers. Facebooks offer both ads and pages designed to grab the attention and promote the customer to act. All the while giving the business flexibility to work across many devices without the need for a massive IT department.

For those looking to get started with Facebook, the first thing we suggest is, to begin with, a free Facebook Page. This is an online home for your business outside of your website. Pages allow all those eyes scrolling their feeds to discover your business as a digital storefront. As well, the setup process for doing this is very simple, and Facebook even offers a step-by-step setup guide. As well as a page manager, you will have access to the Pages Manager App, which allows you to connect and interact with your page while on the go. It also allows you to keep your business separate from your personal Facebook.

Some of the benefits of a page are it is simple and free. It only takes a few minutes to have your page up and going. The page also is very versatile, with many tools that are also free to help you grow your business and achieve your goals based on your business model. Some of these tools include the ability to post pictures, videos, polls, milestones, and engage customers right on your page. Stores allow you to share videos and bring your audience behind the scenes of your business. Allowing them to be more amerced into the experience of what your business is. As well it offers you an inbox for direct communication with your current and potential customers. Additional tools include the ability to set appointments, create events, post jobs, and even post merchandise for sale or link back to your store. Within Facebook's insights, you can optimize your page using the insights tap to overview your page and its engagement and take action to improve your posting and what your community is engaging with and what they are not. The Ad Center is where you can see how your ads are performing across demographics and create ads.

When just getting started, it is important to grow your page by simply inviting customers and friends to like your page—letting them know that they can support you by simply interacting with your posts and sharing your content. These two actions help to build your reputation across the platform and help you to begin to be noticed by Facebook's fancy algorithm and pushed higher in the search results and your customer's feeds.

Additionally, you can always run an ad to get more Page likes. People who like your page will receive notifications when you publish updates, and staying on top of posting to your page helps the SEO to know that this page is active. It is recommended that you post 2 to 3 times per day. These posts can be prescheduled through Facebook's publishing tools. As you grow the engagement of your page, you will see that there is a difference between your organic growth and that of paid growth. Organic growth is people who are already interested and want to support you. Growing organically, you can do by making people aware of your brand. You can share your page on your personal timeline and ask for friends and family to share in their news feeds.

This is not the only way to grow, and the best and most effective way is to be active. Just like your current location, your business needs to increase engagement to drive more customers. This means as an admin of your page or the advertiser of the page, and you should comment on other's posts in as many groups or other Facebook Pages as you can. You can have your business join groups and pages. Sharing more content on your page or in the story also increases your creditability but shows the algorithm that people are connecting with you and want to see your page. Management of your communications in your inbox, if it's a customer who wants to know about a product, solve a problem, or looking for a job. This communication helps to drive your ranking. Furthermore, the use of live video or video of any kind tends to push you further ahead in ranking with Facebook's algorithm. So it is time to get brave and hop out from behind the camera to share your passion for your business.

While these organic was are amazing to grow your business Facebook also offers many great ways to use target ad campaigns. You can actually run an ad that will appear not only on Facebook but also on Instagram, Messenger, and in the outside Facebook audience.

Let's first look at boosting posts from your page. A boosted post is an ad that you create from a post you made on your Facebook Page. This type of action helps you to get more people to react and comment on the post. It also can help you reach people who are likely looking for your page, and currently have not followed you yet. An example of this could be Smoothie Mart made a post about the fresh new fruit options and made a slide show of all the fruits available. Boosting this post could help Smoothie Mart reach people who like smoothies but haven't liked Smoothie Mart yet.

Another option would be to drive people to your website. Through a call-to-action button on your post, you can send people specifically to any page on your website. The call to action button could even send people directly to your phone and have them call you directly for bookings or any number of call-to-action items.

The next type of paid post is to promote your page. If your goal is to increase the number of fans or those who like your page, you can run an ad specifically designed for that goal in mind.

Promote your local business is another type of strategies that Facebook Ads has for business. If you are a locally owned business, you can run an ad that specifically only targets those around you. This can help you spread awareness of a promotion or something that is important within your community.

Once your page has over 100 fans is when we suggest you start looking at insights to optimize your ad targeting. Page insight is very powerful, and it can help you to have a greater understanding of who the people are that like your page and help you to increase your overall page engagement. Do your fans engage more with the video? Do they engage more with Photos? Do they like to see you live? All of these things can be found through your insights and can help you to achieve your business goals. It is essential to understand when they are online. It is easy to get lost down in their feed if you are posting after they have gone to bed or way too early in the morning. Through using your insight tools, you can see when your fans are most active and schedule your posts if you are not available to publish at that time manually.

So now you have an overview of all the things related to Facebook. I know it can seem overwhelming, so I pulled together these tips to help you kick start your Facebook marketing strategy.

1. Goals – Set a goal; this will be your roadmap and is necessary for you to be able to see where you are going, and if your strategy is successful.
2. Know who your audience is – you have to understand who you are connecting with knowing your breakdown male/female age are all important to understand what the best methods will be to attract more of these people. OR to help you target different demographics that you haven't tapped into.
3. Be Proactive – Engage with your audience through discussion conversation and sharing. As a brand, you cannot forget that it is social, and that means you have to interact with them. Your social media marketer should not put engagement on the back burner. It should be a priority.
4. Use the Scheduler – Creating content every day can be brutal on any marketing person. However, Facebook's publishing tools are always improving and a freeway for you to block out content for days or weeks at a time. Most businesses know what's happening for the next 30, 60, 90 days and can create content to schedule out and reduce stress around big launches.
5. Decide which Ad strategy is best for you. Where do you live? Do you live on your social network? Do you want to push customers to your website? Think carefully about where you want to spend that marketing budget.
6. Do you have employees? These are the people that can be your biggest cheerleaders and advocates. When you get your employees to share things from

your social pages, they are more engaged, and you build brand awareness.

7. Know your results – the last thing to keep in mind is your return on the investment. What is your ROI, did the strategy work did you drive more sales, make more connections, grow your business? If you are not looking at the results and determining their worth, then how do you know if you are moving forward on your ultimate roadmap?

4.2 Instagram

If you have not put Instagram on your radar when it comes to social media marketing, it is definitely time to open that door and explore the platform. The popularity of Instagram has continued to grow at a rapid rate. The social platform reports having greater than 500 million active users, moving the needle to make it larger than Pinterest, Snapchat, and Twitter. It is also important to note that 60% of Instagram users visit the platform daily, with 55% of those who are young adults visit more than once a day.

So how do you set your brand up for success with Instagram? It all begins with making sure your account is set up correctly. This all begins with making sure your account is set up as a business account. By converting your brand's account to a business account, you have accessibility to valuable tools, similar to that of which you read about in our Facebook portion, such as insights.

Okay, so just how do you strategically make your account as successful as possible? The most basic thing you start with is your account username. Make sure when you create your business account, you sign up with a business email so that your Instagram is not automatically linked with your Facebook personal account. Under the full name, you will enter your Business name; this makes it, so your business profile is easy to recognize by visitors. Keep in mind that your User name is different from your account name. It is important to match that to the other accounts associated with your brand. So if you already have a Facebook and its name is "Bob's Big Bands," then you would want to have that same name for your Instagram. Consistency across platforms helps to keep things simple for you. It also helps to make it easy for your customers to find you on their favorite networks. When picking the user name for your account, it is a great idea to make sure it is easy to recognize. If your desired username is taken, try to keep the first part of your username your business name.

Now let's talk about optimizing your account. Everything begins with your profile picture. It is the first impression new visitors will get; we suggest that you keep your profile picture consistent across you your social networks;

this just makes for consistency in your company branding and is a great visual marker. Many organizations use a logo or hero item, a familiar image as their profile pictures. Understand that your profile picture will automatically be cropped into a circle, so it is important to leave room around the corners of your image.

The next section is the bio, which is limited to only 150-characters maximum. The goal is to be direct with why people should follow you and who you are. There's no need to use hashtags here because Instagram bios are not searchable. So just keep it simple and feel free to encourage customers to visit your site or use a specific hashtag when posting about your business. Another key part of Instagram happens in your bio, and the bio is actually the only place you can feature a clickable URL to drive traffic externally. Since this is the only place you can use an external link, we suggest using something like linktr.ee to be able to share multiple links with one simple link. For example, you may want a link to your contact page, your store, a specific promotion really the sky's the limit when you combine a Linktr.ee account with your bio link. On the plus side, Linktr.ee offers a free service for you to try it out.

Let get into a little more in-depth on your settings for Instagram when you click on the three stacked lines (often referred to as the hamburger menu) in the upper right-hand corner of your profile. You will see a link for settings at the bottom of the screen. There are a lot of things you can control in your settings.

Let's start by looking at the settings for comments under your privacy. To do this, click the hamburger menu, then privacy, then click comments. This allows you to hide keywords or phrases. To do this, you need to add those specific phrases into your setting under the manual filter. This is important if you know that there are specific terms or words that your audience will find offensive. If you cannot think of anything, we highly encourage; at a minimum, you turn on the setting for "Hide Offensive Comments." This will help to automatically filter comments that Instagram's algorithm deems offensive.

Now let's look at how your story settings are sharing across the platform. To do this, click the hamburger menu, then privacy, then click story. Make sure the setting for Allow Message Replies to be set to Everyone and that you are archiving your story.

You will also want to save yourself time and set up your sharing settings on Instagram. This allows your followers to share your story as well allows you to share your story automatically to your Facebook Business Story. Stories are a huge part of social marketing, and customers and clients love to interact and participate in your stories. As well they love to see the behind the scenes work of your business.

One thing that many do not realize is that you can have multiple Instagram accounts without having to log in and out. You can actually have up to five accounts and switch between them without having to log in and out, which is great for switching from your business to your personal account.

So those are the basics for setting up your account now let's talk about the types of posts you can make on Instagram. Content is what Instagram is all about; the more engagement, the better. Instagram allows you to post stores, videos, and photos.

The most common and widely used type of post is photos or images. When posting images, it is important to show your brand's variety. This allows your customers to see how diverse and engages your followers in different aspects of your business. It is also important to remember that Instagram users are seeking out authentic posts; they are not interested in standard advertisements or flyers. The best way to

It's also a great idea to repost things that your employees have shared. You can get great content right from them. Chances are if you have employees they are posting to Instagram, the key thing here is just sure to tag the original poster so you can give them credit. This is possibly the easiest way to engage your audience with your brand. It also fosters a bond between you and your employees. So much like sharing your employee's posts, you can also do the same with reposting your fans and followers posts that you have been tagged in. This is where having a specific hashtag for your brand can come in handy. This type of posting not only provides amazing free content for you, but it also allows the original poster a feel-good and shows you truly care and appreciate your customers. To share these types of posts, just simply screenshot and crop the image then share it. Always be sure to give credit to the original poster.

If your brand is one that can offer educational posts. Definitely, it is a great way to build up your followers. Typically, this is done with video, but it could also be a series of photos too; just quick instructions that are easy to follow.

Another type of post and one that is well known at boosting your follows is influencer pots. These are typically posted that use the fame of a well-known public figure or celebrity using your products or interacting with your audience. One of the biggest benefits of influencer posts is getting the attention of their audience.

Brands also use motivational posts to grow their followers. This can be a combination of a visual and a quote of an uplifting message. These types of posts are excellent at amplifying your brand's values and encouraging your audience. There are some great apps in the marketplace like Typic that can help you add photos with text and stay consistent with your brand.

I mentioned earlier about keywords in the section about Google and how they are useful in other areas of your business. Instagram is one of those places where key phrases and words are very important. This process is called hashtagging. Hashtags have literally taken over the digital world. The term specifically refers to keyword phrases or keywords that are spelled without spaces and start with a pound (#) sign. Their popularity began on Twitter, but it has quickly melded over into other social platforms and now found frequently all over the digital world.

Knowing that in excess of 80 million photos are being shared daily on Instagram, it is no surprise that there needed to be a simple way to get noticed, which is where hashtags fill the gap. Instagram has made it simple to find tagged content and users with just simply searching for a hashtag, which means it is essential for businesses to make them part of their marketing strategy. Understanding how the search process works can be helpful in creating a good strategy for your marketing. When a user searches for a phrase or word, the results are shown as top, places, hashtags, and accounts that include that keyword Suppose I research for coffee. As I click on the tabs across the top, I can see the top results, results for accounts, the top hashtags for coffee, and then to places for coffee. All of which provide me with different information for my marketing needs and allow me to gain access to different users that might be seeing out my products if I were to say a coffee shop. You can create hashtags in any number of ways using emojis, words, numbers; just remember that they cannot have spaces.

So how do you choose the best hashtags for your posts? Well, there are many ways, and one I suggest you use is the free one we already discussed, and that is Google Keyword Planner. It allows you to see the hashtags are most popular not just on Instagram but everywhere. As well you can also do hashtag research right within Instagram and plan your hashtags that way too. Just simply click the tab that says tags, and it will show you a list with the hashtag and how many posts are associated with that post. So, for example, when I look at #coffee, I can see that there are over 66 million posts. It is best to use a blend of hashtags when you post to increase your pots reach and relevance. There is also nothing wrong with creating your own branded hashtag. Many brands have rolled out their own hashtags and found great success. This is also where you can get your audience to engage by using a branded hashtag. Oreo did a great job with this when they brought out Oreo thins and dubbed the hashtag #OreoThins sometimes simple is better.

The last thing to remember when it comes to hashtags is to avoid being spammy. They should be natural in the caption, and the average brand uses two to three hashtags per post.

The strategy is a big part of marketing regardless of the platform, and a solid strategy is necessary for social media, just like it is in any other aspect of your business. So when you begin to branch out into Instagram, it is important to set your goals for Instagram. So here are a few things that you can do to get yourself kicked off in the right direction.

1. Set a goal – Why are you on Instagram? There is no right answer here if you want to sell products to set a sales goal. If you want to grow awareness for your brand, set a goal for that growth. Regardless of the reason, be able to define your goal before you begin. This way you can measure your performance and see your return on the investment

2. Know your Instagram audience – use popular events or interesting hashtags that are meaningful to your business and see who is engaging with them. Check out their profiles, look at your competitor's followers, and find your niche audience.

3. Plan – Plan your calendar; there is something to be said with configuring an editorial calendar. Brands, on average, post a minimum of six images a week. This is well over 300 posts at the end of the year; with that frequency, it can be hard to stay fresh and keep track of things you might have

previously posted. Planning your posts out and using a service like Planoly will help to keep your feed fresh and you on track.

4. Stay consistent with your brand – when you post randomly or disjointed content, it can confuse your audience. This can also cause you to actually lose flowers. So keep your brand consistent if you are bold and playful, then stay that way if you are positive and uplifting make sure that rings through all your branding and posts.

5. Growth!!! – This takes time and lots of energy. Whatever you do --- DO NOT BUY followers. This purchase is not worth it, they will not drive your engagement, and your pots will not be seen. The things you should do is make sure your username is recognizable and searchable so people can find you. Make sure your Instagram is optimized, which is what we started out with this section. Then follow accounts that relate or would be of interest to your business. A community of like-minded people can open you up to influencers who might also enjoy your products, and you enjoy theirs.

6. Convert followers to dollars – As you establish a dedicated base, you will begin to be able to see your work paying off, and you can start to implement the process of promotions, contests, teasers, and even live launches!

4.3 YouTube

Video has become an important player in the social media marketing world. This means we cannot leave out the most well-known video platform across the world YouTube. The video actually accounts for upwards of 69% of all internet traffic, and that number is still growing. So how do you grab your part of the YouTube marketing traffic? It, like any other platform, begins with a strategy for your brand.

Like with the other social networking strategies, you want to start off with creating a YouTube channel for your brand. The names should be consistent across your platforms to make it easy for your customers, fans, followers, and new subscribers to find you.

Content is the next key factor, and while we didn't touch on it a lot, it is important for all social networking sites. Your content should be relevant and target your audience. Remember this key thing people want to know what is in it for them, not what you have to sell. They want to know how it will benefit their life or how they can gain enjoyment or entertainment.

So let's look at the different types of videos you can create –

1. Trailer videos – These are great for targeting new subscribers, and they allow you to introduce

yourself or brand. They should consist of three basic parts an introduction, the benefit, and a call-to-action.

2. Statistics Videos – numbers are a great way to build your creditability. They also make your brand look reliable and organized. Customers love to see relevant market research, and your brand conducting research means you are staying up with trends. These videos are really easy to shoot and really only require simple graphics and tools like adobe premiere or iMovie, and you can share your data with your audience.

3. Testimonials – When your customers give testimonials about their experience, it helps to build your brand's creditability. These videos should include an introduction, before the scenario, how they found your brand, and how the brand changed them.

4. Questions and Answers – Simple Q&A sessions you have received from your website are another great video to share. It helps your followers know that you are a source to rely on.

5. How To's – YouTube is the spot for DIY and people to find out how to do a huge array of things. Creating a how-to video for your brand will help you to build trust and become a source for their needs when they are looking for more information on your products or services.

Let's look at some of the tools that YouTube marketers need to know when creating content. Everything begins with a title, and it should be engaging and envelope that must-see feeling. This is the way you are going to grab their attention and get them to click your title and watch your content. This also goes back to sneaking in those keywords we have talked about throughout the book. They are a great way to get noticed. The use of "Best-of" or "how-to" titles also rank high when attracting people to content. Titles should also be relatively short between 41 and 70 characters.

The next key thing to do is set up your YouTube SEO. We talked about SEO a bit in the section on google, and it flows over into our YouTube results. When you do a google search, one of the tabs that pop up at the top is video, so any given how-to product video has the potential to show up in the search results. As long as you've set your SEO! So, to increase that SEO traffic to your channel you need to include –

1. Title and descriptions with keywords.
2. As well saying your keywords in your video helps YouTube understand what the video is about.
3. Encourage your subscribers and followers to like the video; this will help you to rank higher in the algorithm YouTube uses.
4. Categories – These are a way to organize your videos so that YouTube knows who to show your videos to.
5. Tags – Tags, just like keywords or hashtags, are very important to target your audience on YouTube. You can add as many tags as you want;

just be sure they make sense with your brand or product.

The next important thing is to use customized thumbnails. This is a simple yet effective tactic to promote your channel and get people to click on your videos. Often the default screenshot that YouTube grabs is not the best look. To upload your own custom thumbnail, you can use programs like Canva to create custom images.

4.4 Emerging Networks

There are always new and exciting things happening in the tech world, and that does not limit itself to the world of computers and cell phones. Social networks have grown, as well. Each year there are new emerging networks that start to make traction to compete with the bigger networks. A few I found notable enough to mention here. The first is TikTok; it is capturing the world and has well over surpassed 1.5 billion downloads and growing every day. This popular new app is very viral and allows your brand to connect in a new way with millennials and Gen Z. TikTok is all about sharing 15-second snippet videos set to music from popular artists and labels. It is all about the viewing experience and completely community-led, collaborative, and a great channel to consider for your brand's marketing strategy.

Another emergent is Lasso social connection. It is Facebook's attempt to take on TikTok and offers many of the same features that TikTok has. It uses an in-app camera for you to customize your content and overlay music. The algorithm curates a feed and recommendations fro vides that users can tap through the ever-popular hashtags to view content. You must have an Instagram or Facebook account to use Lasso. You can even cross-post to stories when you find videos you want to share.

The next social network is Snapchat, with over 300 million active users monthly brands are finding that it can be a powerful tool to use as well. Snapchat now allows brands to create SnapAds, Sponsor Geofilters, Sponsor lenses, and use their Discover feature. While the discover feature is currently out of the reach of many small businesses, it is good to know it's out there, and you can still focus on growing your following by sharing your business through your companies snaps.

Chapter 5

Open up to the world with WordPress

In our world, visibility is paramount. Who we are, what we want to communicate, these are elements at the basis of any form of interaction, and, therefore, of business. To express our values and to show our presence, the web is a formidable tool and manage a website is for everyone.

5.1 Writing sites with HTML

If we were a shop, the ease of reaching a website with a simple, intriguing name would put us in the same street where all the high fashion shops and jewelers are. Once the customer finds us on the web and visits our site, we have a great opportunity, and we must try to make the most out of it. First of all, we must catch their attention. There is no limit to the imagination, creativity, and content that we can insert. Too bad that a web page is not as easy to organize as writing a word document is. A web page is the layout of a program, which is HTML, javascript, PHP, and creating websites requires some knowledge in the IT field. Perhaps, precisely for this reason, there has always been a certain diffidence in sharing information via the web. In fact, many web pages ended up becoming advertising pages, shop windows, or pages full of bugs and computer flaws. Whoever turned to an IT to create a site might have avoided paying maintenance contracts. Meanwhile, professional websites were getting more and more beautiful. Mind you, HTML is all in all a fairly simple language that makes it easy to add content and images, but all in all quite poor in terms of graphics and dynamism.

It is evident that many people have lost a direct relationship with the web world, with the immediate sharing of information, their experiences, their point of view. Until blogs were born. The concept of the blog has revolutionized the interface of websites, as it represents a page with static and dynamic parts. The user can create an elegant and stable structure -or ask a computer scientist to do it-, that will, at the same time, have simple access and where it is possible to add constantly updated contents that integrate and are harmonized in the main interface. With this philosophy, Wordpress represents one of the most popular CMS (Content Management System) in the world. When I was a boy, together with a close friend of mine, Alex, we developed some websites together after school. At the time, it was easy to get a shared web domain, and we could upload something that belonged to us, a list of useful or interesting sites, some information to share. Even then we already liked feeling important and being able to organize our fantasy world in a small part of the web. We worked mainly in HTML, using some small javascript application to make the site easier to navigate.

Although it was simple enough to build small websites, the limit of HTML is that very few things can be done, and the graphics are very simplified. The alternative to building a design website and exploiting the skills of a pool of computer scientists is limited by the lack of willingness and the inclination to maintain a fully upgradeable platform. In the past, in fact, you could often see abandoned websites with missing images, their links no longer being updated. Those pages were beautiful, organized by specialized centers, but then the maintenance cost was not sustainable, and therefore they had remained unmanaged. The Internet is a very powerful resource, but it must allow us to simply manage things.

5.2 Why did I switch to WordPress?

I entered the WordPress world thanks to a friend who introduced me to it and to the developer community, and I am very satisfied, both for the possibility of being back to creating captivating web pages that I can develop easily and because there are many interfaces available and plugins that increase their potential in a striking way and allow you to easily create just about anything. WordPress thus presents itself as the ideal platform, which can be developed in a simple way even without costs, and allows you to create websites that are stable from an IT point of view and captivating from a graphic point of view. I remember some time ago that I had known a computer scientist able to develop websites with Python, a very refined programming language. The web page was fantastic, but once the website had been developed, no one was able to update it anymore. The moral of the story? There are more suitable tools to represent exactly what you want to represent with tools that are available and for which there is no need to intervene on the code.

The construction of a website and the design of the same website are two concepts that we can consider similar but are often complementary. A graphic designer wants to make the colors, the layout, the structure of the graphic interface attractive, exciting, or convey exactly the message that is in the intention of our commercial proposal. Being able to easily add content is the greatest desire of a content manager, the possibility of being able to intervene on graphics is the ambition of a graphic designer. Will these two worlds ever meet? And above all, will a third person, the client, who often has the ambition to intervene on content and graphics, ever be able to join it? We will make some examples with the online tools available on a site. For the development of websites, I prefer to use of a particular theme that allows me to represent anything; thanks to a fairly simple interface, I can easily intervene on the graphics while maintaining the simplicity of the CMS concept, bypassing the limits of many themes that respect the structure of the main configuration.

Why is it important to simplify content creation and testing of graphical interfaces? We want to influence our world today, be it real or virtual. Even the development of a web page requires a fairly varied level of expertise. You need to buy the domain, manage the web space on a shared server or on a dedicated server, activate a database, install the CMS files and then enter the user interface and start building the structure, pages, and articles. The structure is generally composed of a header, a footer, a main menu, other secondary menus and a central body which can be a static page or a dynamic page. Generally, at this point, a theme is chosen, the preconfigured version is followed and the contents are added. The contents can be static or dynamic: we can build static pages or configure a blog, where we can add very easily articles that integrate based on the type of target on the main screen. In this way, our web page can be updated constantly, while still maintaining its main structure. After introducing me to the knowledge of WordPress, my friend showed me his preferred solution: using one of the paid themes, which, will then allow you to do much more. Essentially, this trick allows you to overcome even the limitations imposed by the structure of a CMS designed to be a blog.

If you visit the website of this book, you will find some examples that show the performance and characteristics of the theme that I now use regularly. The advantage, however, is essentially to contravene the limitations of your blog. For example, if I wanted to make the blog become part of the main web page, I could include it in any position and with the targets, I could create different blogs for different topics within the same environment. If I wanted the main menu not to be the same for all the pages of the site, but only for some pages, I would be able to create secondary menus and insert them in any part of the site. But an additional advantage is that when wanting to know exactly where the images go, or how the graphics are to be built, I can overcome the CMS schemes and move, adapting my design down to the single pixel without the need to intervene on the code. So, with basic computer skills, I can easily manage websites with even different objectives without having to give up some functions, and with the advantage of creating dynamic sites quickly and without structure errors. Today, however, the phenomenon of a huge number of smartphones entering the digital world meant an increasing number of people visiting the site from mobile devices and tablets. WordPress allows us to see what the different layouts will be, making navigation possible even from smartphones and iPhones.

5.3 Focusing on content and graphics

The great advantage of not being forced to enter a code to create web pages allows me to focus on content and graphics rather than language, and I can dedicate that time to easily configure more and more pages and sites so that the customer is fully satisfied. Today, the content has become important again; in a period in which very few books are read is actually one in which we read a *lot of stuff*. But reading, or to put it better, the use of the informative material, takes place through ever new forms. Every day, we read newspapers, watch the progress of the stock exchange, check emails, read the news from our friends and acquaintances on social networks, update our personal profile on LinkedIn or share a post, perhaps adding a comment. The information material that we are able to manage today is much wider than it used to be, even if newspapers are bought less and less. Today, the same information spreads in a different way, sometimes also through social networks, also through fake news. And nevertheless, the content, be it a post, a video, or a podcast, is simple to share through different channels. The figure of the Content Manager has become extremely important nowadays, as the contents must be managed, for their aim is inducing action in the person receiving it; in fact, our way of communicating is also changing because, if mediated through social media, it is conditioned by the fact of obtaining an interaction. Let's try to think of a phrase: "today it is raining as well". If we wanted to objectively tell our mother, we would tell her that it is raining today, but if we wanted to post this content on a social network we would have to find the point of view, the idea to arouse interest. We could write, for example: "If it continues like this, Noah should begin to careen his Ark" Talking to the net changes the way we communicate: we become storytellers, build a character around our figure: we can be lovers of good food, caring fathers, politically correct people, conspiracy theorists, the braggarts.

Today, when writing content, no one wants to add <p><a href="https://www.> and a lot of other codes; we focus on our own creativity and the image of ourselves we want to share with the world. Even for a company, the contents to be developed are strategic elements of the business, especially in an era in which those who listen or read can interact with our messages and contents. Let's leave controversies aside: they turn out to be important when writing provocative messages, but for now, we shall focus on the realization of our project. Today, the same person could be a computer scientist and a web designer, as it has become easier to add content and create design pages without going through the source code. Hence, we can focus on the message, the meaning of what we want to create, the emotions it gives. Once again, digital tools become simple and allow us to do things on our own, or at least in the setting part, with a little study we can do very beautiful things. In the live part of this book, I will show you how you can easily create content. Below, we try to look in more detail at the theme I use to work with WordPress

5.4 A business case: DIVI

The great advantage of WordPress lies in the fact that you can create modern and functional web pages without spending money and focus mainly on content rather than scripts. There are many themes and plugins that increase the potential of the CMS. After learning how to use WordPress and add content, the same friend of mine who introduced me to use it advised me to buy a theme developed by Elegant Themes, DIVI. I know my friend well, and I trusted him. I didn't want to spend money, but I must admit that his advice was valid. Why? Generally, WordPress is developed to simplify the website creation procedures as it prepares a header, the main menu, a secondary menu, a footer, and a static or dynamic page that includes the articles that we write in our blog. We can alternate static pages and a dynamic page where the mere introduction of an article allows you to keep content up to date very easily. Furthermore, the structure of the pages and of the blog is quite rigid, not very easy to modify. We should then enter our code, but at this point, we will lose the advantage of simplicity. DIVI does much more. First of all, it allows you to configure the page exactly as we want it. There is no longer a distinction between a static page and a blog, as both can exist within the same page. There are no limitations to creating menus, adding other blogs, creating your e-commerce. Each page can have a completely different look and for this, you need only one database. Essentially DIVI allows you to create your page exactly as you would like it, and great attention has been paid to the creation of columns and spaces that can be

95

formatted at our convenience. There is basically no limitation to continue working with our blog, and we can express our graphic skills and create our website exactly as we would have drawn it on a sheet of paper. This clearly opens up great spaces to those who design websites commissioned by others, because they always manage to satisfy their customers as there are no graphic limitations. And in addition to this, DIVI allows us to create dynamic content that makes our web page attractive and modern in a very simple way. We can then create our complete web page and simultaneously add our landing pages, or take advantage of even a single domain to create many different sites that meet different needs. Even I, who am not a programmer, was finally able to create the website exactly as I would have liked it.

5.5 The web page and the information ecosystem

We are going to conclude this chapter with an extremely important aspect of content management: the information ecosystem. What exactly is the information ecosystem, and why do we need to make sure that information is distributed and built around a unique project capable of transmitting value? Today, our ability to learn is no longer linear. At school, one had to study from page x to page y, and that was what our school work consisted of. Today, if we want to deepen a topic we are faced with a learning path, which could be different for each of us. The path we take has become multidimensional thanks to hyperlinks, the revolutionary concept that started the internet. Through a hyperlink, we can move from one part of the web to another, but also within a website, or a web content; we can move and investigate exactly the topics of our interest. When creating our website, we should take this into account.

Those who visit it are living an experience, which is part of the customer experience that leads the client to the purchase of products or services. The path that our customer will take within the site (which can be properly traced with the analytics tools applicable to WordPress as Plugin) is also the way our customer experiences when visiting our shop. For example, if we had a physical store and there were areas where no one enters, we would probably try to change the assortment to make that sector more interesting. Similarly, a customer who enters our website gets to know our values, our mission, is informed about our testimonials, and ultimately decides whether to buy from us or exit the website without spending money. With the most recent analytics tools, it is possible to understand if our potential customer visited our website a second time, how many times he did that, with what frequency. The structure of the site itself must be connected with the other social channels of our project. Those who know us will learn to look for us on the internet: they will see our videos on YouTube, our advertising on Facebook, and will eventually get to one of our landing pages. Once there (and we cover this topic in the next chapter) they will already have become our customers, hopefully people that have learned to know us and appreciate what we do, for our values, that they probably share. Of course, our product will have a high price, but that will be justified by the virtue of the value that we are distributing to our customers. But we know that they followed us, and appreciate what we do and how we do it. For them, we will have a unique offer that will cement our relationship forever. We have begun to understand as of now how the information ecosystem will be the starting point for building our sales funnel.

Chapter 6

Funnel Management

6.1 Managing Leads

So you have implemented your social media strategy, and now you are growing leads the next step is finding a way to manage that lead and bridge the gap between marketing and sales.

The first step in this process is understanding your leads. Knowing the demographic, behaviors (blog readers, Snapchat, video), and the source. A brand needs to really get to know the mindset of the place these leads came from.

The next step is to generate and collect information about your leads; some brands use lead-capture forms and give access to premium content. Others use tracking tokens to see where the links were clicked from. You can also use your marketing analytics or insights to determine how people are finding you.

Third, you will score these leads, and not all leads are worth your time and effort. The greater the score, the more likely you will be to convert. These leads are often time-sensitive, so it is key to have a normal practice fo following up and keeping them active. Cold leads may need a bit more nurturing and guidance to get them to buy into your brand.

Pass the leads to your sales team, and the lead has been gathered and scored now it is time for sales to move the ball. Sales are where you will begin to see the ROI on the investments you made through your marketing tactics.

6.2 Mailing Lists

Email marking is one of the highest ROI's brands have. Those brands with good email strategy build strong, loyal lists. As you build your lists, it is important to make them healthy. There are many moving parts of developing good lists, but the ones with the greatest importance are churn and engagement.

As with anything, your brand sends out the goal is to create and drive customer engagement. It is a critical part of ensuring the campaign drives results. If no one opens the email or no one comments on the post, then it could be a wasted opportunity.

So how do we move forward well we learn from our churn? Churn is a term that refers to the people leaving your list through reporting as spam, unsubscribing, not opening emails, or their address bounces (meaning it was a bad email address). These people are not engaging, or they are actively disengaging from you. The typical churn rate is around 83%; this means that only 17% of emails are actually making it to the target audience. Understand that some churn is inevitable, and the best practice is to keep rejuvenating your list to manage the churn rate.

So how do you develop a strategy to keep your churn down and grow your list here are some great practices for your email lists management. Begin by making subscribers feel welcome. The first contact with a subscriber sometimes can be the first interaction with your brand. This is best done by sending an automated welcome message email or series of emails that are triggered by their opt-in. This initial email should welcome them to your brand and ask them to "whitelist" your email in their address book to keep you out of their spam folder.

The next thing to do is keep your lists clean; just like anything else, if your desk is full of junk, it can be much harder to get work done. Your email lists are much the same. Our suggestion is to do a list cleaning about twice a year, often around the times a year, or if you happen to notice a spice in bounce rates. So how do you clean your lists? Simple first remove any duplicate addresses, remove or fix any addresses with typos, update or remove an invalid address, and delete emails from bounces. Honestly, do not be concerned if you remove a lot of invalid emails addressed, people, change jobs, move and get new addresses frequently. However, by removing these addresses from your list is important because it reduces the number of bounces that hurt your reputation with the email servers.

Once you have purged your email list, it is time to re-engage or remove old contacts. An unengaged contact that has not opened your email is not doing you any services. You have a few options you can work to re-engage that subscriber, or you can purge them since they are not helping your sender reputation or the return on your investment. Re-engagement is an excellent way to boost subscribers that are lagging; we always suggest creating a campaign to reach back to the subscriber before letting them go forever.

It is also important to make unsubscribing to your email easy. I know this sounds crazy when you want people to subscribe so you can grow your reach with your brand. However, having unengaged people subscribed to your list hurts your deliverable rate. Those who unsubscribe were most often not engaged anyway, and it is better to spend your valuable time and marketing dollars on those already engaging in with your brand.

The last thing to touch on is never to buy lists. This practice is actually illegal, and you could end up with a lot of backlashes from violating the CAN-SPAM and end up with fines in excess of $16,000 for emails that were not sent properly—additionally purchased or rented lits are often not of any quality that makes them worthy of your brand. They often consist of spam traps and email addresses that are not valid. Do not fall for it!

6.3 Automatic Sales Funnels

Sales funnels are a great process to add to your business. They are one of the core concepts of digital marketing. The process is a multi-step process that moves prospective browsers into purchasers. So the funnel works like this –

1. Create your content and pull in leads
2. Lead magnets – this is the call to action something you want them to do but also often something that they want to get in return. Like a discount code, e-book, webinar, access to podcast
3. Split the funnel – The beauty of an automated funnel is you do not have to work it every day, but using split tests, you can make sure it is still

functioning. So you may use a Facebook post with a free e-book, or you might use an email with a code for a discount.

Setting up these funnels does require some work, but in the end, you can build your brand awareness and save yourself time and effort by allowing this to be completed seamlessly without your need for constant interaction.

You can see these types of ads on Facebook constantly for brands trying to do social coaching or help you grow your business. The join my webinar on this day at this time. This is an example of a sales funnel that webinar is pre-recorded, and all the emails and links leading up to it are part of the workflow to make these things happen.

6.4 Software Solutions

So we have covered many things over the pages of this book. The last concept that we need to look at is some software that can make your life as a social media marketer easier. These tools are designed to help you reach your social media marketing goals regardless of your business size.

Many small to medium size businesses choose to use self-servicing social media marketing tools as part management style. The list below is are not the only option when it comes to social media marketing; these were just the top picks we felt were most helpful and well rounded.

Sprout Social – this software provides the ability to see reports for your social accounts and monitor keywords in the search stream. You can also schedule your content and use its publishing system to manage social accounts on the go.

Hootsuite – has become known as a leader in the social media marketing management world. It has a robust offering for publishing and monitoring to even offering the ability for team collaboration.

AgoraPulse – this software is a toolkit for Twitter, Facebook, and Instagram and supports the ability to host contests, monitoring of platforms, CRM, and customizable reporting. Everything funnels into what looks like an email conversation of social data and fans.

Buffer – was actually a pioneer in the social media publishing world and has continued to grow in popularity across platforms. This service allows you to publish and schedule all social networks with the exception of Instagram.

While these are just a few of the options when it comes to software and your social media marketing, it is important to take a close look at each before committing to one. Many of these services and others not listed offer a free trial period for you to test drive the service and see how it works for you and your brand.

6.5 Final Comments

Social media marketing is an ever-evolving and changing industry. It is important to remember the key things of staying true to your brand and growing your customers that fit within your brand. As you have learned from this chapter, you are now equipped with a wealth of knowledge to grow your brand in ways you may not have considered before. The next step is to go out and create content and find your niche in the social world.

Chapter 7

Digital tools for companies

In this chapter, we will address one of the central themes of this book, namely, how to exploit the Internet and the digital cloud that surrounds us to our advantage to try to obtain advantages in our work. At the end of the chapter, we will make further considerations. It is not enough for us to be satisfied with the advantages offered by the digital world: we want to exploit the automation of the digital world to provide services and to generate profits. But let's start looking at existing services and try to understand how we can make the best use of them for our business.

7.1 The digital cloud is already at our service

Why do we have to put our trust on the internet today? Compared to that of a few years ago, our world has changed a lot. The" victims" of these changes weren't the services that already existed, such as post offices, shops, groceries, butchers, hairdressers. They mainly concerned the digital world, or rather, they concerned all those goods and services that could easily be converted to digital services. Is being an entrepreneur today as difficult as it was before? In a certain sense, yes, if we approach the world as we would have approached years ago. The situation is different if we want to exploit the new digital world or get help from digital services on the internet. In this case the subject changes completely.

Even outside of business, our lives have changed. We use smartphones to access information from the ether that come to our aid at any time of the day or night. Iin most cases, this help is free or, in any case, a real transaction is not foreseen. For example, if we ask Google Maps to show us the way to reach a specific address, we have probably never been to that place before, but we trust that what has been elaborated by the algorithm will allow us to choose the means of transport that is more convenient for us to use. We can ask for an opinion on a restaurant and know what the customers of that restaurant have said, and we can, therefore, access information accumulated for years that allow us to be able to better interpret whether that place will be right for us, or not. We can call a taxi and even if we have no idea where we are, the application will inform the nearest driver, which will reach us in a set time. From a smartphone, we can book a ticket to the cinema, the theater, an exhibition, we can join a meetup, we can create a meetup ourselves, organize a meeting on a theme with people we don't know, but who are perhaps interested in the theme we have proposed for the meeting.

7.2 Choose the correct strategy for growth

What strategies exist online? Surely there are many, but which ones can work for growth? Today, we have many tools at our service, perhaps even more than before, and each of these tools can be used for free or on a limited budget. But be careful: these tools are constantly changing! Perhaps the difficulty to penetrate the market is not so much to open an online company but to be very clear on what you want to do and which KPIs we need to keep in mind, in order to drive our business. In order to do this, it is necessary even before starting an activity, whatever it is to understand what is worth doing on the market. Obviously, we will not be forced to do the same thing all our lives, but it is still important to have an idea of where to start. Before choosing one, and before I invest my time and money, I already have useful tools for testing at hand. Before falling in love with our idea, let's try to think with the mind of a person that we have identified as our ideal customer. People buy to solve a specific problem or to feel satisfied.

I don't think there are other reasons. Purchases performed to feel satisfied only concern our private life, like food, a holiday, or a dress. Most of the cases, if people open their wallets, or type in their credit card number is basically to solve a problem. Indeed, the vast majority of the purchases that we can control are those made because you have an issue and want to solve it, and this is anything but simple, as solving a problem means moving from a state of chaos to a state of order or, to put it cosmologically, to go from a cloudy sky to a clear blue one. Solving a problem means for our client means to put the solution directly in their hands. And that's why many businesses fail: they don't think about the solution, but just focus on the product, even if today, it is less important than it once was. What counts nowadays is the result we will obtain. What can we do to solve our customer's problems? How do we make our client feel that if he comes with us the problem will be solved? The only real way that I can think of is to let him have a taste of our offer, to start solving the problem for free. This is what Microsoft did with Windows. They proposed their solution, which was light years more innovative than DOS and allowed us to work with multiple windows, on multiple open documents that could be open simultaneously. And since that solution was really appreciated, Microsoft let people install it on their PCs, even for free. In this way, people got used to using it and knew that this solution was advantageous for dealing with and solving many of the problems of the digital office. A digital product was born to solve a problem. In order to convince one to buy our solution, we have two possibilities, at this point: they could get some advice by someone else who has already successfully adopted that solution -but consider that this is not going to happen if

111

you are starting your activity from scratch- or you could give your customer the opportunity to enter your network and taste our product, to be convinced that only with it, will they be able to solve its problem. Then, another fundamental aspect of today's business comes into play: is the product we offer also simple to use? A minimalist approach is important not so much for the future, when people who have bought from us and are comfortable with our product may also be willing to spend more time or to take courses to fully learn its functionality. It is essential for the initial product testing as well: even when we are going to release a free sample of our product, we must develop a prototype that is simple to handle. Paradoxically, the free sample is more important than the paid product, for it is what allows our customers to enter the funnel, to begin to get closer to our solution, to get used to our presence on the market." if the free solution is so valid, let alone what the paid solution will be". We must be able to give our very best even before people buy from us if we want them to think like this. We shall strive to convince customers that our first and true goal is to try to solve an important problem, a problem that belongs to the world, or to our portion of the world to our niche, and make sure that in offering our solution, including the free sample, we are already effectively starting to offer valid solutions. This will allow us at a later time to dare to ask for something more from the people who have also become our customers for free, and above all let's get used to giving the best of ourselves even if no one is yet buying. Only this authenticity will allow us to obtain commercial results.

7.3 What if we chose to outsource?

Companies with many employees are difficult to manage. What is the best number of employees to have? My point of view? Not too few, not too many. Having only a few workers means not being able to grow, not having resources available and not being able to grow as fast as the market may require, or our competitors are doing. On the other hand, hiring too many employees means having high costs, and you should be sure that everybody works in a synergistic way. The right choice lies in the middle: having an indispensable number of employees, treating them well, paying them well like real professionals, continuously keeping them updated, and training them in the best way. Then, just let the money do what we don't want or don't know how to do. Today the economy is shared, and as we have learned to understand, everything that is shared is also cheaper, because competition increases. So we can take advantage of some outsourcing websites and delegate the parts that we don't know how to do or that take up a lot of time to them. The network will work with us on the realization of our project. There are many people with experience in the field of design, in information technology, and that are able to deal with special software applications. Or rather, we can post a job ad ourselves, offer a price and accept applications for that type of job. These services are reducing poverty in developing countries, helping people who have lost their jobs, or just need to work from home. The only things they need are a computer, an internet connection and some good skills, and if you start to outsource jobs, this also allows you to enter into a series of stable relationships with the professionals we trust most because we have tested their services. The shared economy allows us to delegate important tasks to professionals whose value is recognized and tracked.

On the other side, what is more valuable than time? We can get more money, but surely we cannot get more time. In some cases, suppose we want to do everything by ourselves, it may happen that we will never succeed in business just because this means too much work to be done.

A recommendation (that is worth a lot of money!): earn to believe in outsourcing. Many times, we have ideas and we have to deal with the fact that if the project has already been taken over by another person, even if the result will probably be different from what we had in mind. Be careful, if we exclude those situations, in which the work has just been performed badly, I can instead assure that there are times when a different eye can see things that we are not able to see. I had commissioned a logo for an application, and I did not like what was proposed to me at all: it was different from how I imagined it. I asked the unlucky freelancer working for me to modify it many times to try to adapt it to what I had in mind. A couple of days passed, and I realized that the first logo that had been developed was the best, and that embodied the meaning of my message completely. The freelancer had been really good and I hadn't behaved well!

Let's give a look to some of the most used websites where you can easily find the right professionals to who outsource the job you don't want to do by yourself.

Fiverr

Fiverr is one of the worlds largest marketplaces to hire freelancers for your projects, offering a large field of industrial online applications. You can search among very inexpensive tasks (starting from 5$). It offers different service levels called basic, advanced, premium, and clear communication of the delivery time with a running countdown. The number of revisions that can be performeds unlimited in some cases, but please keep in mind my own experience, don't drive the freelancer crazy while your job is already perfect!

Upwork

Fiverr is thought for inexpensive and simple jobs, and it can include some more advanced jobs, but if you want to go for a more complete service you may prefer Upwork. On Upwork, you can post a job, describe what is needed to be done and you can decide to pay for the number of hours employed or for the cost of the complete project. Although this choice is arbitrary on the site, I prefer to pay for the whole project. It is not my job to verify how much time you actually spent on your work. I am concerned that the result is in line with my expectations, and for good service received, I am very willing to continue to use the same service at other times.

Freelancer

Over 15 years online, Freelancer represents a long-run solution for small and middle-size outsourcing projects. Crowd favorites are outlined, like website development, logo design, marketing, mobile app development. Most of the categories are related to information technology, but you can get access to other services, some of them are related to technical writing and publishing. As in Upwork, you can post a job and pay for time or for job completion. You will then pay only when you are completely satisfied with the job done.

If you are searching for a Virtual Assistant (VA) on a larger project, then you may get profit from **Zirtual**.

Workhoppers claims to help you find the right person by basing your search on a language-based algorithm that uses artificial intelligence and thus allows you to locate your VA without having to search among hundreds of identical ads.

If you focus more on content production you could choose among **Textbroker**, where you can get professional contents, or The Urban Writers and E Writer Solutions to hire a ghostwriter for a full fiction or non-fiction book.

FreeeUp makes a distinction based on skill level rather than price or person. We choose the level of competence we need before moving forward with further research of the VA.

There are some more web portals if you are not yet satisfied, please reach out to **Toptal**, **Hubstaff**, **Outsourcely**, **PeoplePerHour**, **Workhoppers** ...

However, it is extremely important to maintain control over our assets to ensure our decisions are strategic. Among the topics that we will tackle and keep updated in the live part of this book (following the canon of living books insights), we will discuss how to grow our company online. Here, however, we would like to inform you that it is not the number of hours worked that makes the difference in an online company but the quality of the hours worked. For this reason, we must devote a good part of our time to thinking, exercising, walking, meeting friends, meeting new people, and meanwhile thinking strategically, establishing strategies for hacking the system. Every day we must think about new strategies, understand the needs of the constantly changing minds of people, and we must represent the security that they do not find elsewhere, an anchor in a moving system. People will begin to understand that their problems will be solved with us and without us, the problems will remain there. So we will have to be able to devise ever new and ever more advanced solutions, keeping in mind that many utilities of the digital society are easily available and exploitable in a click.

The time we find, as Proust said, is the time that we have recovered in a programmable economy, the time we will earn in the morning because by opening our dashboard, we will notice that at night someone has already purchased from us from overseas; then, we can have breakfast calmly, we will be able to bring it to our partner in bed, accompany our son to school, devote some time to our fitness, but carving out here and there the opportunity to listen to some podcasts or listen to some audiobooks between workouts. To be entrepreneurs, we will have to be constantly updated on new trends and understand what is at the forefront of the market; we will have to participate in training events with the foresight to imagine the future that will be, with the ability to predict behavior and trends, the desire to anticipate the market, because now this is possible even without moving large capitals. It will be our intelligence to leverage, not our money. And then, we can imagine a different and radiant future, we can go around while the others are in the office to work, or get up an hour later while the others are already in traffic.

We will find hours when supermarkets are deserted, discover wonderful places where people only go during the holidays, and new ideas for our projects in nature, local traditions, culinary specialties, we will corroborate our creativity with innovative ideas. In the evening, we will have terminated our job as other people do. The others will have satisfied their employer. We too will have achieved our results in agreement with our ikigai. Except that, while the others fall asleep on the couch exhausted for another day spent managing the usual problems, we will arrive in the evening full of energy because our work will have been a great energizing game, a great opportunity to see our ideas realized in the world.

Conclusion

In order to improve the mechanisms of our everyday business, we had to examine the reality that has definitely changed in recent years, and will most likely continue to change very quickly. Those who speak of a crisis are probably referring to this taciturn but very fast transition between the old world and the new world. This total instability typical of the liquid society must not distract us from the ultimate goal of our business, which is to build our content online. The importance of content management is growing with new technologies, as the customer experience has become a path that customers start right from the web.

In fact, the typical customer begins his market research on his smartphone or tablet, where they can study the product or service, can receive information, watch videos and tutorials. In the meantime, an idea is being made of which product best expresses their vision of the world, or simply meets their needs. it is still early to buy, we must wait for the path to be completed, first of all in the minds of our customers who must get used to our presence, our values, our valuable contents. Only then will our customers begin to compare prices and product features. Of course, in some cases, this process is very fast, but especially for the purchase of a service, this process can take a long time, even a few months. And it is precisely in these months that our digital content management will be made explicit. This is the time to set up our funnel, to check our flow of information, to check the success of our online campaigns. Now we have a few more tools and a few more certainties, and the time has come to act. Each of us has skills that can be converted into business branches. Before many of us did not have the money to undertake new markets and remained with the idea, but without the possibility of realizing it. Today, however, thanks to network sharing, we can focus on what we really know how to do and we like to do. For everything else, the internet will help us out.

The project for this book will continue online. Visit the website:

https://www.lineprofile.net/remote-teams/digital-content

and access updates, tutorials and online content. Don't forget to leave a review, if you liked this book or if you want to comment on the text. Now is the time to act: today digital technology allows us to test ourselves also with tests that we can do by writing the contents of our favorite hobby, for example. We will be able to develop all the aspects that generally concern a real business by talking about how much we like to go fishing, what techniques we use, what tools we use, what are the best times, the secret places, the permits, the appropriate clothing. But please, do not come to me to complain that the digital content project of your fishing hobby has been so successful, that you have decided to take care of it full time! Indeed, let's say this, this would mean that this book, in some way, has been useful to you!

www.ingramcontent.com/pod-product-compliance
Lightning Source LLC
Chambersburg PA
CBHW030704220526
45463CB00005B/1902